# The Gospel According to Abbie Jane Wells

## (A Sampler)

# The Gospel According to Abbie Jane Wells

## (A Sampler)

THE THOMAS MORE PRESS
Chicago, Illinois

Portions of this book first appeared in slightly different form in *The Critic*, Chicago, IL, *The Witness*, Ambler, PA, and *The Inside Passage*, published by the Catholic Diocese of Juneau, Alaska.

ISBN 0-88347-175-2

# DEDICATION

To Dan Herr, who else?
He made this book happen,
and I hope he's satisfied!

# By way of a preface . . .

"Read, mark, and inwardly digest, and see what the Scriptures say to you" are words I heard in church many times. So I took them seriously and started to do just that, and I found that oftentimes the Scriptures said different things to me than they had said and still say to others. And so I wrote these thoughts into notebooks, and into letters, and I would mull them over and discuss them with others on occasion.

It seems to me that it is sheer stupidity to look at the Scriptures through the eyes of the past—only through the eyes of those who lived before this nuclear age, this space age, this jet age, this computer age, this age of fast communication world wide, etc.; as stupid as looking at war in the same old ways of the past, as though a nuclear war would be nothing more than a re-play of past wars, only on a larger scale—to use the thinking of others, and quote the thinking of others from the past, rather than to do our thinking for ourselves.

Just think where we would be if scientists were still using the first theories laid down centuries ago by the top scientists of that day—still trying to make those old theories work because they were afraid to try anything else despite the discoveries and knowledge of the intervening years.

A friend wrote: "Abbie Says" is a possible title, but maybe "Abbie Insists!" would be better. Well, I DO *insist*—I insist that people "Read, mark, and inwardly digest"—and see what the Scriptures say to *them*—look at them through *their* eyes, as I have looked at them through mine.

"Try it. You might like it!"

Abbie Jane Wells
Juneau, Alaska
January 31, 1984

**Abbie Jane Wells**

**I KEEP** wishing that Jesus had kept notebooks during his 40 days in the wilderness and afterward —then maybe we would have more to go on as to what he thought or meant. We tend to think he saw things through our eyes and minds, and it is hard to try to see things through his eyes and mind. He said, "All I have done you shall do and more," and I am beginning to wonder if maybe we are supposed to start with 40 days in the wilderness, as he did, and go on from there, in our own way, thinking things through. I am trying to do my "40 days" now in my own way, and it may take me 40 years! It is certainly taking me a lot longer to think things through than it took Jesus, but then, it might have taken him longer if he had done it in the 20th century, for there are so many more things to think through now than there were in the first century—2000 years worth of more stuff, near-abouts.

\* \* \*

I always wondered what might have happened to the robbed and beaten man after the Good Samaritan had left him. If the innkeeper was out to make an extra buck, he could have put the robbed and beaten man back out beside the highway to see if someone else would have pity and bring him back in to be cared for. He could run one wounded man through many times, getting paid every time someone brought him in, maybe using the same wounded man as long as he lasted.

You can see that the story requires an innkeeper who could be depended on to do what he was paid to do. And it requires a Good Samaritan with money in

9

his pocket, too. What if he had been without funds? Then what would he have done for the wounded man; cared for him himself? Maybe that's why the priest and Levite didn't stop—not because they had no pity but because they had no money to pay an inn-keeper to care for him.

\*   \*   \*

I think one of the reasons so many people shy away from things is that it hurts when anyone suffers a loss. God must hurt all the time—and Jesus, too, and all the company of heaven. Why do people think heaven is peaceful, placid, non-involved with what goes on in the world? Man, when you are in heaven you see it all and feel it all, not just one spot of it. Heaven is where you will become *fully* aware of all that goes on in the world and I am not at all sure that I am going to be able to take that. I'm having prob-lems enough with just the little bit I see and feel here on earth. People are going to have an awful lot of ad-justments to make when they get to heaven, for I doubt it's like most people think it is. Couldn't pos-sibly be.

**YOU KNOW,** the Prodigal Son story ends with the boy's return and the father's open-armed and open-hearted welcome. Everybody usually assumes, "And they all lived happily ever after"—no differences of opinions between the two brothers ever marring the peace and tranquility of the father's house.

But I wonder if it was all that tranquil after young Bud returned? I'll bet it was more peaceful for the father *before* he returned, and for the elder brother, too—no fights or disagreements between the kids to have to mediate. Elder brother got all of Pa's attention while the young'un was gone, now he must share. And the prodigal had lots of adapting back into the ways of his father's household when he returned. (I doubt if the elder brother was much help there.) I am sure that the father was understanding of the fact that even though the prodigal wanted to come back, it would take him a while to get back into the groove. But I imagine it took the elder brother quite awhile before *he* adapted to not being the only son around to help Dad, the only son for the old man to call upon or talk to. Now there were two sons to be considered.

Well, for awhile at least, I'll bet it was anything but the "and they all lived happily ever after" routine, for there was an awful lot of adjusting for all of them to do. Not that Pa hadn't always considered the prodigal a son, even while he was gone, but the boy was now underfoot all the time, and even though the father's welcome was so spontaneously joyous, I'll bet it took him quite a spell to get used to the idea that Sonny Boy was right here at home, to be in on everything.

One of the problems is that so much theology about God the Father is done by men who are fathers in name only. I don't think you can know what being a father is really like until you become a father yourself. The feeling of being a father, or a mother, comes only with experience. You just think you know what it's like and what it's all about until you become one, and then you find out all the nuances and inflections you missed.

That's why we get a different picture of God in the New Testament than in the Old—he was different. He was now a father in his own right, no longer just a proxy father but a father for real. And he learned a lot about fathers and children by becoming a father himself—the ultimate being when he found out how a father—or mother—feels when something bad happens to their child which they are unable to prevent.

ONCE A priest friend said something about John the Baptist's first recognition of Jesus—how he knew who Jesus was the minute he saw him in the desert, like he had had a vision or was told by God—and I said, "Of course he knew who Jesus was! He had always known. His mom, Elizabeth, had told him how he leapt in her womb when she saw Mary. In fact, he had probably heard that story many, many times—we all have a habit of talking forever after about our unusual and breath-taking experiences. Perhaps the first thing Elizabeth told her son John as soon as he was able to understand, and maybe even before that, was about the son of Mary and what had happened the moment she saw Mary.

And Mary told Jesus who his Father was as soon as he was old enough to know. He had to take Mary's word for it, as Joseph did—and as my son and his father have to take my word for who the father of my child is, for only I know what I did with every moment of my life, and I am the only one who knows if I was true to my husband. They had to trust and believe me, without proof. So does every man—no way he can know for sure unless he keeps his wife under lock and key 24 hours a day, unless he trusts her to be faithful so that he has no reason to doubt when she says she is going to have a baby, and he knows he is the father without her proving he is or proving she is faithful, because he trusts her to be faithful.

And speaking of faith and trust—Paul had to have a lot to even let Ananias get near him, even to cure his blindness. For Ananias was one of those Paul had been persecuting and he might have had in mind to get rid of the persecutor for good by doing him in rather than returning his sight (or so Paul might have thought). A lot like George Wallace would have to have a hell of a lot of faith and trust (this is a pre-1976 thought) to let a black person he didn't know get near enough to lay hands on him even if he said he could make George walk again as good as new.

And I'll bet those who crucified Christ—involved in it in any way—steered clear of him during Resurrection days for fear or retaliation. Never could understand those "out to get those who crucified Christ" through their descendents. Christ had 40 days to do any retaliation and he did nothing, so why should his followers down through the ages try to finish something for him that he never started and wasn't about to start? His, "Father, forgive them" from the cross was all-inclusive, unconditional, and without them admitting guilt and begging for forgiveness . . . There were none left unpardoned on either side. He forgave Judas, too, and the disciples for hiding out, and Peter for denying him during the trial and crucifixion.

Jesus did no retaliation after the Resurrection, but the crucifiers didn't know for sure that he wouldn't, so they must have kept a low profile. It is sad that Jesus' followers have tried to retaliate ever since— they don't see that retaliation wasn't something he ever thought of doing. And much blood has been shed down through the ages by people "doing for Jesus" what he doesn't want done.

**Abbie Jane Wells**

It's like the people who support boycotts whole-
heartedly when it is Chavez doing it, but scream to
high heaven about the dastardly Arabs using a boycott. I dislike boycotts intensely. I think they are as
violent as hell. An economic squeeze hurts. A boycott is an excommunication from the marketplace,
and I wish the Church would give up all excommuni-
cations, including boycotts, or else support boycotts
as legitimate a means for the Arabs as they say it is
for Chavez.

A boycott is oppressive to those being boycotted
and to those caught in between. As we have examined war and the means used not justified by the
ends, so I think we must examine the means used by
unions—and count the costs laid, against the gains
made, and see how much it costs others, the "innocent bystanders," for the gains made by union
members. The cost to the public is getting greater
and greater.

When teachers strike, it makes me wonder if education is what they say it is. If it is, the teachers
should have the reasoning power to settle all differences without having to resort to the means it doesn't
take an education to use. If an education doesn't
equip your mind so that you can reason and not have
to use the strikes and picketing and boycotts—if the
educated can't reason—then why get an education?
Teachers who strike make the public wonder if an
education is worth the bother, for they are using the
means the uneducated have to use—and with all that
"education" they've got going for them, too.

**I FIND** this new church "doctrine," "Love your enemies and boycott hell out of them," neither Christian nor nonviolent, no matter how "gently" done. Wars maybe served their purpose in days gone by, and maybe so did strikes and picketings and boycotts, but we are more reasonable people now (or we claim to be) than we used to be, and should find other means which are of the "come let us reason together" variety, except the educated are now the ones who seem to have lost their ability to reason, as teachers' strikes and busings and boycotts show. To ask parents to send children into any violent confrontation is an abomination. I don't care what the reason is, "education" is not worth doing this to them. Making the children have to take what they have to take in the name of education is giving them an education in violence far greater than they get from watching violence on TV. And it is being done to them by adults who won't reason out their differences.

Jacques Ellul bothers me, for I can't understand what he says. I guess he, like many others, thinks this is a Time of God's Abandonment.

I don't think this is a time of God's "abandonment." I think it is a time when God has really untied the apron strings from his grown-up children, as he must have done with his own grown-up Son. I don't think "Jesus obeyed his Father until death," like God was calling all the shots and doing all the thinking for him.

Parents—good parents—"let go" of their children when they become adults, and good parents let go completely. They don't "abandon" the children when they untie the apron strings, they just stop putting their two cents worth in like their offspring were still children instead of adults.

And so it is with God, I think.

And so it was with Joseph. There came a time when he quit teaching Jesus to be a carpenter because Jesus had become a full-fledged carpenter and could work right alongside the old man without being told how to hammer in each nail and saw every board.

People act like we haven't grown and matured a bit since God—or our parents—took us by the hand and led us where we must go. This is one of the failings that priests often have. They so often talk to the parishioners in the same manner as they talk to children, explaining the faith like the parishioners were children, too, and a wee bit simple-minded at that. Priests keep the "flock" in a mentally retarded and spiritually retarded state whenever they do this— talking down to adults as if they didn't know anything.

**THAT DREAM** the wise men had, to return home by a different way—the Bible doesn't say it was a dream from God as was Joseph's dream to take the child and his mother to Egypt. Why does everyone assume that the wise men's dream was from God, too?

And have you ever looked at it from Herod's point of view? Here's a King who sees wise men bearing gifts, but not to him. That alone would make a King mighty mad, regardless of who the gifts were for. And then they promise to return and tell him what they found and where—and they don't. They go back on their word, and that, too, would make a King mighty mad. The wise men treated Herod the way nobody in their right mind would treat a King—shabbily.

Another thing. If Herod had really wanted to find the Babe, wouldn't he have sent one of his own men that he trusted to follow the wise men, so they could come back and tell him where they went, etc., rather than depend wholly on these strangers to be men of their word and come back?

Have you ever wondered what might have happened if the wise men had gone back to Herod, and the questions Herod would have asked about any King, new-born or not? Like: "How many soldiers does he have?"—"Well, there were two, and one of them was his mother." "How many servants?"—"Well, there were two, and one of them was his mother." "How many followers?"—"Well, there were two, and one of them was his mother." "What's his palace like? How well fortified?"—"Well, it's a stable, with no fortifications."

This is a threat? To any King?

Could be that if the wise men had gone back to Herod, things might have been different.

Besides, the shepherds went and were changed by what they saw. The wise men went and they were changed. Herod, who said he wanted to go, too, was prevented from going. Maybe this made him a changed man, too—a *more* violent man. 'Tis possible, had Herod seen the Babe, he might have been changed by what he saw, into a *less* violent, maybe even nonviolent, man.

And I wonder how the wise men felt when they heard about the slaughter of the innocents. Did they wonder among themselves, "Maybe if we had disregarded that dream and gone back maybe something we could have said to Herod would have simmered him down so he wouldn't have struck out so violently and blindly in a rage."

It always makes me mad when people don't do what they say they will do, unless they have made clear that maybe they won't. And I wonder if perhaps Herod was as mad at the wise men as he was at anyone—taking it out on the innocent babes as much because he couldn't get at the wise men as because he couldn't get to the Christ Child—as "Child Abuse" often is. Taking gifts to the King into whose country you come is the thing to do—always has been the thing to do; and keeping your word to the King has always been the thing to do, too. The wise men did neither. They weren't as "wise" as people think. You just don't do this sort of thing to a King, no way, no how.

# Paul or Jesus?

I am so tired of what "St. Paul said" being used as proof text for what the Church should be. The Church, which claims to be the Bride of Christ, is more enamoured with Paul than it is faithful to its one and only—and *that* spells adultery in my book.

No man on earth is going to let his wife run his household according to what some other man says— but that is what the "Bride of Christ" does every time it goes with what Paul says.

Paul may have spoken to his generation—but Jesus speaks to all generations. I do hope that at the Second Coming, surrounded by heavenly hosts, that Paul is one of them. I can't wait to see 20th century woman tie into him! And 20th century man, too, in a few instances.

Let's get with Jesus and leave Paul back in the first century to rest in peace, where he should be left.

**Abbie Jane Wells**

# Another Nominee for "New Adam"

For 19 centuries Christians have been using and relying on first century thinking. Well, I happen to think that it is time for us to interpret for ourselves what Jesus meant—for we do not live in the first century—nor is our knowledge limited to that or to what St. Paul says.

Paul said Jesus was the "New Adam," but there were two at creation and Paul makes no mention of the "New Eve"—and that is where the male-oriented and male-dominated Church has been content to leave it.

Were I to develop a concept of the "New Adam," I would have to include a "New Eve."

For that, I think no one can beat Mary. And since Adam was not the Son of Eve, but was her consort, I would have to choose Joseph for my "New Adam," and Jesus would be the "New Cain," the non-violent Cain, the Cain with his head screwed on right.

Just recently, I was thinking of God between the Conception and the Nativity, with Mary seven months pregnant, having to leave her care up to Joseph. And I would imagine God did a fair share of worrying, knowing all the things that can happen to a pregnant woman and her child in utero—things that certainly aren't the will of God but are mishappenings of nature or accidents.

And I can just see inexperienced Joseph—not a midwife and certainly not an obstetrician—in charge of things. At Christmas I picture him, eyes raised to heaven, holding in his hands the afterbirth, saying,

21

"Oh, God, what do I do with this?" Joseph not only got to care for the birth, he was also in charge of the clean-up detail. And he got to cook the Christmas dinner, too, whatever it was.

Much is made of Paul supporting himself at tent and sail making. Well, Joseph supported himself— and two others besides.

I prefer seeing Jesus through the eyes and words of Matthew, Mark, Luke and John rather than through the eyes and words of Paul. When I write my book of "theology," I think I will title it "And I Could Be Wrong!" I am not sure that I see things rightly, only that I see things differently. What woman doesn't? And men aren't going to like the way I see things. At least, most aren't. . . . Right now I am doing the years in Egypt with Mary and Joseph—and I have to stick it out as long as they did in Egypt, I think.

**Abbie Jane Wells**

**YOU KNOW,** Mary and Joseph were the first liberated female and male. Mary said her "yes" without first running to ask Joseph's permission, or any rabbi's permission. She said "YES" all by herself, without input from any man, not even Joseph. She thought for herself, all by herself.

And Joseph, too, thought for himself, all by himself. He didn't run to ask the rabbi what "tradition" said he should do about this pregnant woman, for he knew damn well what tradition said. But Joseph didn't ask, and did what he thought was right for him to do, and I doubt if that got him any accolades from the religious establishment of his day.

I have wondered for a long time if God picked the couple Mary and Joseph as much because of the quality of Joseph as for the quality of Mary. Joseph was an uncommonly fine man, willing to believe when there was nothing to see to believe in, willing to go it alone with no community of support.

Of course, I have learned something from Paul—not much that I can use in the 20th century—but I've learned a lot about first century man. The domineering kind. The converted stone-throwers. And I've learned a lot from Joseph—most of which I can use in the 20th century. Joseph wasn't a stone-thrower. He bucked the "tradition" of stoning the wife whose extra-curricular activities left her pregnant.

The sign I have mounted on the side of the refrigerator in front of which I write would have been a perfect sign for Mary and Joseph:

There are no rules
about leaping into
The New because
Nobody has ever
been there

We have things to deal with today that Paul and his
crew never heard of, things even the early 20th century thinkers and theologians never heard of, things
that Jesus didn't have to deal with, even if he knew
about them.

First and foremost is that damnable split atom we
have to live with and try to control, and the nuclear
arms race. In the garden Jesus said one sword was
enough. He wasn't starting an arms race with Caesar. Caesar's arms race then dealt with swords; today
Caesar's arms race deals with a nuclear stockpile.

And I could go on and on. The church is living in
the 20th century just like the rest of us, and has to
deal with 20th century problems—using the precepts
of Jesus to base its actions on. But it seems more content to try to make Paul's "theories" work today as
they may have worked in the first century.

Jesus never said anything about homosexuality
being a no-no; so today we have the church still de-
bating the subject because Paul was against it. Paul
may not have "preached another gospel than that of
the apostolic communities" but I think he preached a
different one from Jesus. I guess this argument could
go on forever and probably will. . . .

**Abbie Jane Wells**

# Wondering: With Mary and Joseph

I often think of what Elizabeth's spontaneous response must have meant to Mary and Joseph. Here was one more person besides themselves who knew—and they hadn't told her.

It had to be true, then, and not a figment of their imagination. For there must have been times, at the very first, when they sort of had doubts themselves—like maybe it was just a dream. It always helps loads if just one other person is "with you"—the proof needed. For when only one or two know, people might think it is something they dreamed up between themselves. But if a third person also knows—and they didn't tell them—then it is more than just something they dreamed up.

I once asked a friend, "You know what I think Joseph's first thought was when he saw Mary returning from her three months with Elizabeth?" He said "No." And I said, "I'll bet he thought, 'Oh, God! I didn't know she would look so pregnant! Conceived of the Spirit—I thought it would be like spirit, not like flesh—and here she looks just as pregnant as any woman!'"

For Mary probably already had a bit of a waddle to her walk, and maybe she was already showing a bit. I have had friends who had a bit of a pot belly at two months even. . . .

I have often thought of Mary and Joseph talking about the coming baby: "And who do you suppose it will look like? Mother or Father, or a combination?" (You know, as prospective parents do.) And Mary and Joseph wondering if the baby looked like his Father would they be able even to stand to look at it, as they remember the stories from the Old Testament of how one cannot gaze right at God. Would they be able to take the sight of the Son of God? Fortunately, the son looked more like his mother than like his Father. But there was no way to know that before he was born.

And they must have been worried about such things as, "Will we be able to handle the Child? Are we competent to raise this Child?" And stuff like that. There was no book on "The Proper Care and Feeding of the Son of God" for them to bone up on.

I almost knew by heart the "Better Homes and Gardens Baby Book" (from mid '40s) by the time my son was born. I was so afraid I wouldn't know what to do with this baby when I got it, and it must have been much worse for Mary than for me. She knew she was just an ordinary woman, having an Extraordinary Child—and she must have wondered if she was woman enough and if Joseph was man enough, to be up to it.

People talk about praying for what they want. Well, I am quite sure that what Mary got wasn't in answer to her prayer! A woman would have to be out of her mind to pray, "Oh, Lord conceive of me Thy only Son . . ." Perhaps some did who didn't have the foggiest notion of what they were asking for—or all that would be entailed in getting what they prayed for.

I have listened to people who pray for everything in the book—parking spots, clear weather for picnics—anything and everything—and when they get what they want, they proudly proclaim how God answered their prayer.

And then the day comes, and it always comes, when what they are praying for is a matter of life and death and they don't get it, and then they wonder what is wrong with them and what is wrong with God that he didn't answer this prayer like he did the others—like they *thought* he answered the others. So they doubt themselves and they doubt God. . . .

**I WONDER** how much shunning Mary and Joseph got in Nazareth? After all, they weren't married yet, and Mary was pregnant. I wonder how much company they had, or if they had any, from their religious community and from family and old friends?

I wonder if by the time they left for Bethlehem, Joseph was all Mary had left. I wonder if she gradually learned how to be alone as people turned away—first one and then another—so that she was used to being alone before she got to Egypt.

Perhaps Egypt was not so bad after all, for there she did not have to see people who had turned away and left her. Maybe she was ready to be alone in Egypt because she had learned how to be alone in Nazareth.

Perhaps Joseph had to take her to Bethlehem in those last stages of pregnancy. I wonder if all who went to Bethlehem, or anywhere else, to be enrolled for taxes, also had their wives along if they were pregnant, just like Joseph did, because there was no one to leave her with in Nazareth who would care for her like he would? I have always wondered about Mary's mother and father, who would let their daughter go off on this trip without seeing that there was someone along to assist her with the birthing. If Joseph couldn't afford to take along a midwife, I would think her relatives would see that there was one along—or if they couldn't afford it either, that one of the women would go along herself. What happened to all of Mary's women friends and relatives? Was this of no concern to them?

Perhaps Egypt was a pleasant change for Mary—

for there she would not have to see people who no longer spoke to her or had anything to do with her because they didn't believe her like Joseph did— because they said, "She sure can't pull the wool over our eyes like she did over Joseph's—she can't con us as she did Joseph, and Joseph can't con us either!"

If a woman today were to give birth to the Daughter of God, and that is a possibility, if not a probability (I don't think God is content to be the Father of only a Son and not of a Daughter, too), I wonder how much support she would have during her pregnancy, and after, from her church community? From her family? Friends? Town? Country?

**WHAT** if a woman alone—without a man like Joseph she was betrothed to—were to be the woman God picked to bear his Daughter? I wonder if she could go it alone from start to finish? I doubt if I could, even with an unearned income like I have to pay the costs. I guess a woman could if she had to, but it sure would help, I think, if she had a man like Joseph around to give her a hand. I wonder if Mary would have been able to get the baby to Egypt without Joseph? I doubt she could have made it. Even today, with unearned income, it would be almost impossible without someone to help, without someone to believe as Joseph believed, in you and what you were doing for God. . . .

And I wonder if Joseph ever got to enrolling for the census before they left Bethlehem in a hurry? With all he had to do, it is easy to see that getting enrolled for taxes may not have been number one on his list— especially after the baby was born—for here was a baby that Joseph KNEW was special, even if nobody else in Bethlehem did, save for Mary.

I have been thinking of Joseph and all he had on his mind during that trip to Egypt—not the least of which would be traveling with those Christmas gifts—gold, frankincense, myrrh—and worrying about getting robbed, maybe even killed, in the desert. Then there was the daily grind of providing food and shelter—not only shelter for the night but from the midday heat. That was sure no "pleasure trip" for any of 'em.

Much later, I recall that two of the apostles tried, with the help of their mom, to reserve the two seats of honor at the table in heaven for themselves. Well *I* think those seats were reserved by God at the Conception for Mary and Joseph. And if I am right, that must be the shocker of heaven for many, many men and women—a woman yet, in one of them; and Joseph yet, NOT one of the apostles, in the other. Well, just in seniority alone, Mary and Joseph put in more time living with Jesus. And Joseph had to live with him in his trade, too, answering questions about all of his business practices. Imagine ANY business man having to do that today! Even in a one-man or one-woman business, it wouldn't be easy if you wanted to make a buck or two extra on the bottom line.

A prophet like Jesus on the payroll would cut down on the profits, I would imagine. No business man, nor business woman, either, in his/her right mind would want Jesus on his/her premises, much less as right-hand man. But Joseph put in a good many years at his carpenter's bench with Jesus right there asking questions.

I think Joseph is the example for the laity of "living with Jesus." Perhaps the apostles are the examples for the priestly ones. But Joseph is the example par excellence for those of us who live and deal in the world's market places.

Well, I see Mary and Joseph as the "New Eve" and "New Adam," and I see Mary and Joseph in the honor seats of heaven's banquet table—and I see it all starting with the Conception rather than with the Resurrection. As I see it, the Conception is proof that God is reconciled to his earthly kids. The Conception is the vehicle of Reconciliation between God and humanity. We have learned the hard way that having a baby rarely ever reconciles estranged man and woman. We have learned the hard way that having a baby won't hardly ever save a marriage that is nothing but estrangement. But I think God knew that all the time—2000 years, more or less, before humanity found it out. I think God had to be reconciled with creation before the Conception, in order to have a child by one of them—for that's the only way having a child works out well or successfully.

A baby conceived of love won't keep the love a going concern, either. Estrangements can come even after you have a baby together in love. It looks like maybe that is what has happened between God and Creation lots of times.

Well anyway, these are just my suppositions, and my nose won't be out of joint if I happen to be completely wrong.

**Abbie Jane Wells**

# Bethlehem (plus 2 years, 9 months)

Dear Folks,

It is quite an experience to be an Israelite living among the Egyptians—trying to explain to the Boy about the history that informs our religious celebrations—trying to explain to him why the Egyptians don't do like we do—and at almost 3 years of age he can sure ask questions!

Trying to explain Passover will be worse next year than it was last, for he will ask more questions. How to tell him so he doesn't throw it up to the children he plays with, so that he doesn't call them names because of what their ancestors did to our ancestors? Joseph and I talk long and hard about how to do it so as not to downgrade the people we live amongst and the children the Boy plays with.

I don't think I wrote in any of my letters about what a load off our shoulders it is to no longer have those priceless gifts the Boy received. As I told you before, Joseph had to sell them in order for us to have something to live on until Joseph found some work. And what a relief it was to no longer have to worry about the gold, frankincense and myrrh being stolen as we did on the trip to Egypt when there was no way to keep them safe from robbers. The thing that probably saved us was the fact that we looked too poor to have anything of value. Instead, everybody felt sorry for us and fed us instead of trying to rob us. We would never have made it if it hadn't been for the people who shared what meager food they had with us.

I have been busy weaving cloth on the loom that Joseph finally made me. So now we all have clothes that aren't one patch on top of another. It took Joseph a long time to scrounge enough wood for the loom—wood is so expensive we couldn't buy any. And this place needed so much done to it to make it halfway comfortable.

We were lucky to find this abandoned stable. Many people, especially refugees like us, are having to live in caves. There really isn't enough for the Egyptian poor and hungry, much less us.

Joseph and I are getting ready for the Holy Days, which means more questions from the people we live amongst—and from the Boy. And we will try to answer the questions and do our religious celebrations so as not to carry on the ancestral quarrels. It really is an on-going challenge to try to keep the faith as we would in Israel. We do miss having family and religious community to worship with, and rabbis handy to give us answers when we are not sure what to do, to tell us how to answer the Boy's constant questions. We try our best to explain that "When in Egypt, do as the Egyptians do" isn't the right policy for us.

We look forward to the day when we can return and see you all.

Till then, I send our love,

Mary

**Abbie Jane Wells**

# Mary's Diary

Hallelulah! We're going home to Israel! Joseph just told me this morning that God told him in a dream last night that Herod is dead and it is safe for us to return.

What a relief—at times I have felt like a ghoul waiting for Herod's death, sometimes almost wishing for it, may God forgive me. Sometimes I have thought God had forgotten us and we would have to stay here forever, may God forgive me my doubts—but now this is forgotten and we are getting ready for the trip.

Hallelulah! The Boy may get to have his 4th birthday among his relatives—a real Jewish birthday with Jews instead of a half-way one in this foreign land. I can still hardly believe we're really going home. Is this only a dream I shall awaken from?

I must write the folks and tell them—and tell them about the Boy asking the questions at the Passover seder—about all the questions the Boy asks—how good that soon he can ask others besides Joseph and me about his heritage. It is time he had rabbis to question and talk with, not just two like us who know so little.

Joseph has a carpentering job he has to finish—bless that good man for not just walking off the job and leaving it unfinished because I want to leave right away—today! It wouldn't be right for him to do that—and we do need the money to buy enough food for the journey.

There is one advantage to being as poor as we are—we sure don't have much to pack to carry—and as soon as the news gets around there will be someone who is having to live with family in cramped quarters who will be wanting the house. It isn't much, but it is a house, a *furnished house* yet—ready for another small family to move in.

The Boy isn't as happy as I am—he hates to leave his Egyptian playmates—but he is picking up so many things from them that sometimes he acts almost more Egyptian than Jewish and I don't know how to handle this without causing him unhappiness, for he does love all the children here and their parents.

I keep pinching myself to see if I am only dreaming we're going home to Israel! And day dreaming about our reunion with all our loved ones—and showing off the Boy to them!

Well, I better stop this day dreaming and write the folks that we are leaving for Israel in about a week; as soon as Joseph finishes this job, so they can get ready for us! The trip shouldn't be as hard going back as it was coming to Egypt—with the Boy almost four and able to walk as fast as I can almost—and with me in better physical shape. Believe me—a trip right after childbirth is sure no picnic!

I wonder again, as I often do, about Bethlehem—and the days of mourning that must take place there each year—mourning the massacre of the innocent babies, right after we celebrate the Boy's birthday. I wish I might visit the mothers and fathers and try to comfort them, but I am sure I am the last one who could give them comfort. With my Son alive and well, I feel they would resent me offering *them* sympathy and trying to comfort them, so I guess we better not go through Bethlehem on our way back to Nazareth—the Boy will just have to take our description of his birthplace and the stable, and make-do with that without seeing it. It would be cruel to the grieving and mourning parents to take him there. . . .

"JESUS the same, yesterday, today and tomorrow." Well, if that be true, then when he returns he's going to be just as Jewish as he was on the first go-around—and what will the Church do if he says, as he did before, "I would have Passover with my friends"? Will the Church send him to the nearest Jewish community or synagogue? Will the Jews recognize him as the Messiah on the second go-around while the Church turns its back on the Christ because he is Jewish?

The institutional Church which has stripped all the Jewishness from its services, customs, practices, celebrates a Christ who is Jewish. No wonder the Church doesn't know what to do with him, really—and no wonder the institutional Church seems about as empty a shell as a non-Jewish Jesus is.

If the bread and wine of the Eucharist is transformed into real body and blood, then each Eucharist is like a minute transfusion—a symbolic transfusion of Jewish body and blood—and the more Eucharists a person partakes to become like Christ, the more Jewish he/she becomes by transfusion—or should become, in thinking as well as in body and blood.

The Church should do such a transfusion in its practices, customs, services—a re-Judaizing gradually, perhaps in as minute doses—but as constant—as the Eucharist is celebrated.

If the story of the Prodigal Son is used as a symbol for Biblical faiths—the young son who took his inheritance and left the father's house being the younger Biblical faith; the elder brother who stayed home being the older Biblical faith—the younger son

Christianity, the elder son Judaism—the younger son returned to father's house, to where elder brother was, not vice versa.

And 'tis true, Big Bud wasn't exactly overjoyed at the return of the Prodigal Son—and the Jews might not be overjoyed if the Christian Church re-Judaized itself—to say nothing of an awful lot of Christians—but the Church better do something towards making itself into something Jesus will recognize and feel comfortable in when he returns as Jewish as ever—and it better do it so that its members and clergy don't turn their backs on the Jewish Christ. And what if Jesus brings his mom and Joseph along in that "cloud of heavenly hosts"? It was a *Jewish* Holy Family who lived in the First Century, not a "Christian" one. Mary was a Jewish mother—as Jewish as they come—not the sanitized Christian version.

The institutional religious establishment of New Testament times didn't think much of Jesus—or Mary and Joseph. Will the institutional church of the late 20th century or the future make the same mistakes in its judgments? Will they recognize him when they see him face to face? The Church will really rip its britches if it insists that he submit to a psychiatric examination *before* it allows him into its pulpits and Eucharists.

We who pray to God in the name of his son, have stripped away the Passover in remembrance of God's mighty act of deliverance from our Church calendars—and yet we expect God to hear and even answer our prayers without question. I wonder how this looks to God—and to his Son?

Christians—some of them—have said God doesn't answer the prayers of Jews—never giving a thought to the fact that if God doesn't hear the prayers, then Christian prayers that are "through Jesus Christ" are useless for Jesus is one of those Jews whose prayers God doesn't hear! How screwed up can Christians get? Pretty damn much, that's for sure, when you strip all the Jewishness from Jesus and the gospel and the Church and the Christian faith.

The Church has a lot to answer for in its downplaying and rejection of the Jewishness of the Christ and the Jewishness of the so-called "Christian" faith and traditions. The Romans destroyed the body of Jesus in crucifixion; the Church destroys the essence of the Jewish Jesus Christ—and I am not sure which is worse in the long run.

**Abbie Jane Wells**

# New Clothes for Easter

What did Christ wear on the first Easter morning? Well—it wasn't "the same old thing," that's for sure! His grave clothes neatly folded in the tomb—his robe gambled for by soldiers at the foot of the cross—what on earth was he to put on for Easter?

At first glance, Mary mistook him for a gardener. Could it be that that was because he was dressed like a gardener? Could it be that a gardener shared his clothes with Jesus—the very first, real-live instance of "I was naked and you clothed me" in post-Resurrection history?

Did Jesus come bursting out of the tomb in his grave clothes just as a gardener went by—and scare the poor gardener half to death? Causing the gardener to say, "Man, you can't go running around like that, you'll scare people half to death. Here, let me give you some of my duds, and you can go back inside to change, so you'll look alive instead of like a corpse?"

Or had Jesus stripped off the grave clothes first, before he burst forth buck-naked (the first "streaker," yet!)—naked as the day he was born, causing a passing gardener to say, "Man, you can't go running around like that, you'll catch a death of cold—and, besides, women come this way often. Here, let me give you some of my clothes, at least enough so that you will be decent"?

'Tis said that Mary was the first one who saw him that first Easter, and fortunately *after* he was dressed to look like a gardener. But maybe not—it must have been the one who gave him the clothes who saw him first, and clothed him—as Joseph had done after he was born; two who fulfilled that "I was naked and you clothed me" during Jesus' time on earth.

The empty womb of birth, and Joseph and Mary clothed him in swaddling clothes. The empty tomb of Resurrection, and someone unknown clothed him so that he looked like a gardener to Mary—someone who saw him before Mary did in order to do this. Well, there's a lot to think about on what effect this had on the one who gave Jesus the clothes to wear on that first Easter. Did he know *who* he was giving the clothes to? Or did he always share his clothes with anyone who needed them? Or was this the first time? Was it the last time?

Well, anyway, thanks to some unknown person, Jesus was decently clad when Mary came; and he didn't scare anyone else wearing his grave clothes, or embarrass anyone by wearing nothing at all. The one to whom we never give a thought—or a "Thanks!"—the unknown who provided Jesus with the clothes he wore on Easter, deserves some recognition—so here it is belatedly, with my "Thanks!"

Abbie Jane Wells

# Contradictions

Jesus' "Except you become as children"—and "a little child shall lead them," as opposed to Paul's "when I became a man I put away childish things."

Jesus said nothing—for or against homosexuality—while Paul says it's a no-no.

Jesus said nary a word about "charismatic gifts"—and Paul plugged them.

Well, that will do for starters. 'Tis said that the Epistles were written long before the Gospels were—and I have often wondered if maybe the gospels were written after, and because, the gospel writers had read some of Paul's epistles and thought, "Better set the record straight and get down on papyrus the story as *we* know it."

The way *I* see it, the best way to read Acts and the Epistles is with, "Now where did Jesus say this or do this?" in mind and what can't be verified in Acts and the Epistles by Jesus' words and deeds, can be taken or left alone, as one sees fit. But many people do the opposite: *anything* that Paul said is taken as gospel truth for all time, while people pick and choose among what Jesus said and did, and leave anything and everything behind that they don't find real comfortable to live with.

Jesus says, "Man/woman cannot serve two masters." Paul says, "Let every man be subject to the government authorities . . ." "Let every woman be subject to her husband's authority . . ." or words to that effect—which, with God, gives man and single woman two masters to serve, and married women *three!* Yet Jesus' "Man/woman cannot serve two masters; either he/she will love the one and hate the other or vice versa" still stands—and you can't do it Jesus' way and Paul's way at one and the same time—that is also "serving two masters" and it can't be done without being a waffler.

Jesus said "Blessed are the peacemakers" nary a word did he say on "Blessed are the warmakers"— yet some Christians today write such things as "we need not disagree, however on our need for a dedicated military" with a straight face—seemingly unmindful, or at least forgetful, that it was our "dedicated military" who brought us Vietnam— and the fire bombings of Dresden and Hamburg and Tokyo, et al—as well as the atomic bombings of Hiroshima and Nagasaki. It was, and is, a "dedicated military" who brought us napalm and guava bombs in Vietnam—and cluster bombs and all the horrors of "conventional"(?) weapons and war—as well as the possibility of extinction for the human race with nuclear war weaponry. There isn't any group of "dedicated military" more dedicated than the ones at the Pentagon—Wow, are *they* ever "dedicated!"

It is our "dedicated military" who designs and plans and produces *all* the weapons we stockpile and sell abroad to the highest bidders: cluster bombs— napalm—all kinds of other "goodies" for human extinctions less final for all eternity than nuclear abominations. And all this is part and parcel of any "need for a dedicated military" that some Christians say "we need not disagree, however, on our need for. . . ."

**Abbie Jane Wells**

Well—I beg to disagree with them on that, for you cannot separate the "dedicated military" from the weapons at their disposal—and saying "No" to the nuclear arsenal still leaves the "conventional" ("Conventional?" In whose imagination was *that* term dreamed up?) arsenal intact and in an "approved by Christians" state. Their "seal of approval" on cluster bombs and napalm? Have they ever examined closely what is in the arsenal of our "dedicated military"? Evidently not. Have they ever examined closely what our "dedicated military" is selling abroad to the highest bidders? Evidently not.

Before World War II, we sold scrap iron to Japan, which they turned into the armaments they shot at us. Today our "dedicated military" saves any potential enemies that bother by selling them the finished product, made in America. Even for the military-minded, that should make little sense, and it wouldn't if people weren't so interested in making a fast buck that they don't care how they make it. And Christians are as "good" at this (or as bad) as anyone else.

Well—the Christians who say "we need not disagree, however, on the need for a dedicated military" opens it up—not only for "Christian" military service, but for "Christian" munitions making as well—for any fool knows that a "dedicated military" has got to have weapons—has got to have "conventional"(?) weapons of every description—anything short of nuclear ones, of course—but anything else goes.

"Man cannot serve two masters" but many, many

Christians do try to serve the "dedicated military" while purporting to serve the one who said "Blessed are the peacemakers," seeming to feel, evidently, that somewhere in that statement is a hidden clause that says also "Blessed are the warmakers—the 'dedicated military'."

**Abbie Jane Wells**

**AFTER** the wedding at Cana, I wonder how many offers Jesus got from men who wanted to set him up in the wine-making business? "I'll furnish all the barrels of water you need—and the wine skins—and anything else you need—and you do your trick—and *we* can make a bundle! *We* can corner the market, man!" And I wonder if his name headed the guest list for every wedding or other doings in the area for a time—people thinking they would have to buy less wine (maybe none at all!) if he were around.

Mary said a simple thing, "They are out of wine"— a housewifely remark. And why? Could it be that she already knew what Jesus could do with a little water because he had done it before when *she* had run out of wine when there were guests in the house? Could it be that his words to the effect that his time had not yet come were his way of saying "I'm really not ready to *go public* with my water into wine at the drop of a hat?" Because he figured that people would start wanting him to do this every time he got near? Then he changed his mind, perhaps because he figured he might as well do it for this host as for someone else later—or for Mary when she ran short of wine.

He probably got offers from men out to make a quick buck—he probably got lots of invites to weddings and other festive occasions—people being what they are. And after he fed the 5,000 he was no doubt a popular guest everywhere (after the word got around) with the way he could do wonders with just a smidgeon of food!

Jesus may have gotten some offers to go into the food dispensing business for profit, too. Business men even then were probably always on the lookout for talented young men who could help them beef up their profits—and what a killing Jesus could have made if he had gone into business for himself: feed the hungry at a lower price than anyone else—with some wine-making on the side—and *no* overhead, either!

I wonder how many offers he turned down to make a profit off his miracle-making talents? He could really have made a name for himself—and made a bundle! And don't think the astute business men of that day failed to see this. I doubt if Satan in the desert was the only one to offer him "deals!"

And something for all of us to ponder: When did Jesus and his disciples eat? *Before* they fed the hungry 5,000, so as to have all they wanted first; or *after* the hungry had eaten all they wanted—not real sure, perhaps, that there would be anything left until every one had eaten their fill and the left-overs were gathered up? That's as relevant today as it was then: Do you give unto charity off the top or do you wait until you have everything you think you need and then give off the bottom from what is left over. That's a question for Churches as well as for individuals.

**Abbie Jane Wells**

**AND** there is question hidden in "Love your neighbors as yourself," which well may be: Does this
mean: do for your neighbors as you do for yourself?
Do *as much* for others as you do for yourself and
your own? A 50/50 split between you and yours and
your neighbors? *That* would up the ante on a tithe of
10% for charity—and it would tend to lower the standard of living of the giver while raising that of the
receiver of the charity.

Maybe this is what Jesus had in mind with his "the
poor you will always have with you," the "poor"
being those who have given on a 50/50 split, *after*
they have given, as well as those who received; the
"poor you will always have with you" being *you* as
well as those you have fed and clothed and sheltered,
etc.

Well, this probably isn't an idea whose time has
come even yet—except for people like Dorothy Day
and Mitch Snyder and all the numerous other people
who think and act like they did, and do. But it *is* a
thought to ponder: Does "Love your neighbors as
yourself" mean, for churches as well as for individuals, a 50/50 split between you and yours, and
them? With the addition of "What does the Lord require of me?" it does make good meditational
material in these days of economic stress for the poor
and the hungry and the homeless—of which there
will be increasing numbers this winter as well as in
the days to come.

49

# Somewhere I read:

"The only way one became righteous was to believe that God sacrificed His only begotten Son in order to appease His wrath over what Adam did to the human race."

If that sort of thing is true, which I doubt very much, the churches that preach that sort of doctrine never go beyond that; never follow it to its conclusion, which is that those who "helped" God accomplish this would have to be the first "Saints" of the Church—maybe even the only Saints of the church.

If this were true, then Judas, Pilate, Herod, the chief priests, the crucifiers, etc., were doing "God's work" for him and should be made "Saints"—at least by the churches that preach that sort of stuff, that is.

**Abbie Jane Wells**

**RE: MARTHA**—she really didn't know when she was well off! Mary wouldn't have been worth a cotton-picking damn in the kitchen—not with Jesus in the other room. With her mind on him—not on cooking—trying to overhear what he was saying— Mary would probably have salted everything at least twice—and dropped pots full of food, too. The best thing that happened to busy, busy Martha was that Mary stayed out of the kitchen, out of Martha's busy-with-cooking way.

Did you ever have someone whose head was in the clouds and whose mind was on other things besides cooking, try to help you put together a meal? A meal for unexpected guests? Had Martha known who was coming, and how many, she might have gotten the cooking done early, and then she, too, could have sat with Mary listening to Jesus—like preparing the Sabbath meal ahead so no cooking has to be done on the Sabbath, as Orthodox Jewish housewives are used to doing.

**AND** I'll bet the men listening to Jesus were with Martha, and wished Mary would get the hell out. Women's place was in the kitchen, Martha knew THAT—not sitting in with the men listening to a man talk about things that were supposed to be of interest to only men, not women. Believe you me, Mary would not have gotten away with trying to sit with the men in an Orthodox Synagogue, even with God himself there! Women today don't get by sitting with the male hierarchy either—listening to what they discuss—and there are many women as well as men, just like Martha, who think women have no business trying to barge in with men.

Well, Jesus thought Mary sitting at his feet along with the men, was the right thing for her to do—that she was in the right place for a woman to be—but I'll bet the men agreed with Martha and thought she ought to be in the kitchen, doing "women's work" instead of listening to things of importance—but only to men. THEY could tell Mary and Martha anything THEY thought they should know that Jesus said, later, after he was gone. THEY could interpret his looks and inflections of speech as well as his words, to the women.

And so it still goes many places. But isn't it amazing, really, that God sent his angel to Mary to tell her what she was to do. He didn't tell the angel sent to Joseph to tell Joseph to tell Mary what she was to do.

As Jesus didn't have to tell the men to tell the women in the kitchen what he had said—for Mary, a woman, could tell the women what she had heard

Jesus say—and they could hear it from a woman, not filtered through men's thinking process! . . .

Once, years ago, when I was still active in church affairs, when Bishop Gordon was here and I had been stuck in the kitchen with other church women doing the dinner and the dishes, etc., I said to Bishop Gordon later, "I'm serving notice! I'm not going to be a Martha no more—I'm going to be a Mary and sit in with you boys!" And he looked at me like I had lost my marbles for sure.

And you know what the wrongest thing about the Catholic Bishops' statement on nuclear arms is? It is the fact that there were not an equal number of women sitting with the Bishops, hammering out the statement on the most crucial issue of all time for women and children as well as men. Women should be there IN PERSON, speaking for themselves—and other women and children—having their words listened to FIRST hand and not as they are passed in through bishops—or ignored as not worth passing on. This is NOT the time for women to be told to stick to their knitting and leave it up to the men, either literally or figuratively. Single women as well as mothers must be heard—and children, too. In addition to a children's campaign of writing letters to the president, I think a children's campaign of writing letters to Bishops and the rest of every Church hierarchy, is also in order! And it would be a step in the right direction if American bishops issued the invitation. Maybe even an invitation to women who are not as forward as I at putting in their two cents worth without invitation, too.

**DID GOD** only tell Joseph to get the hell out with the kid and his mom and go to Egypt because Herod was on a rampage—or did God send that message not only to Joseph but to all the fathers of all sons under two years of age in the area, and few if any, except Joseph listened and acted? Did Bethlehem fathers, or fathers who were there with their families for the census, the next morning tell of their "crazy dream" and have the Mrs. say, "Well you're crazy if you think I'm going to pack up and go on a wild goose chase because of some crazy dream you had?"

We say that God is a good God and has concern for *all* his children on earth—even the Russians—and yet we act as if God had no concern at all about the potential slaughter of any child except his own, by Mary, born in Bethlehem long ago—and only warned Joseph to get the hell out and take *his* son to safety. Or else we act as if somehow the Slaughter of the Innocents was a part of God's "plan," or else he wouldn't have "allowed" it to happen.

Joseph might have been able to warn all the other fathers if he had had as much time, and a horse, as Paul Revere, and had had nothing on his mind other than spreading the word to other fathers—who might or might not have believed him.

Surely a good God would see that the message got to all the fathers in the area as well as to Joseph—for God would know what was in Herod's mind, and whose sons were in danger of being slaughtered by the soldiers Herod was sending out in his rampage. As for the wise men's dream to leave the country by another route, I don't see how we can think *that* dream was from God, for that dream made them go back on their word to Herod, which no doubt added to Herod's rage.

But the main thing I wonder; did God warn all the fathers of sons under two years of age as he warned Joseph, but few but Joseph paid any mind to God's message? I would say yes to that—adding that this is par for the course: few men or women pay any mind to God's messages when, or if, it would upset their daily routine or "normal" life.

**ANOTHER** thing I wonder about—as we start thinking about what we will have for our Christmas din-
ners—is what did Joseph fix to feed Mary and
himself on the First Christmas? I think we can safely
rule out a turkey dinner with all the trimmings! (And
who started *that* "Christian" tradition in the first
place?) But what would Joseph be able to cook while
tending to the birthing, etc.? What would they have
carried with them from Nazareth—not only to eat on
the way but to have to eat in Bethlehem? It couldn't
have been anything fresh—and with the crowds in
Bethlehem, there was probably no more fresh food to
be had in the markets than there were rooms to be
had in the inns. So Joseph probably cooked something they brought from Nazareth, something not
perishable, for the first Christmas dinner.

Thinking about this one Christmas six or more
years ago, I cooked a pot of beans, steamed a Polish
sausage and made some cornbread! Though the sausage wasn't kosher such as Joseph would have had, I
figured Joseph *could* have put on a pot of beans to
simmer away while he tended to the birthing and its
clean-up afterwards—or a pot of something that
would need little watching—for he sure had no time
to stuff a turkey even if he could have found one—or
bake pies or plum pudding, that's for sure.

Joseph *could* have simmered a pot of chicken
soup—that would have been better for the new
mother Mary—that is, if he could have found a
chicken handy. He may have had some dried meat
that would have made a nourishing and tasty
stew—but I had no dried meat and did have dried

beans; and I had no kosher sausage but did have
Polish sausage, so I made do with what I had, just as
Joseph must have done on the First Christmas, when
he was kept too busy with the birth, I imagine, to put
together any fancy meal, besides being too poor to afford the makings of any fancy and elaborate meal.

**I WONDER** if the census takers in Bethlehem were local men—or were they sent in by Caesar for this census taking? If they were Bethlehem citizens, I wonder it their sons under two were exempt, or hidden, or gotten out-of-town before Herod's soldiers came looking for the boys under two to kill? Did the Bethlehem citizens who assisted Caesar's census takers—or who housed and fed them if they were from out-of-town—did they lose their sons under two, too? Were they also among the parents who grieved over the slaughter of the Holy Innocents? Did not God also grieve—did not Mary and Joseph also mourn with these grieving parents?

**Abbie Jane Wells**

**WHEN** I am Pope—or Presiding Bishop of the Episcopal Church—when men and women finish seminary, they will get to live what they have learned—apply it—try it on for size—out in the world's market place, until they are 30 years old. And then, if they still want ordination, they will be ordained. I figure that if Jesus didn't figure that he was ready to go out preaching and teaching until *he* was 30, that no ordinary man or woman is going to be either. Jesus tested it all, tried it on for size, as a poor carpenter, *before* he went public with it, and I figure that what was good enough for him will be good enough for the future clergy, when I am running the Church!

And when I am Pope—or Presiding Bishop—I will come out strong for unilateral disarmament for Christians, for Jesus' "one sword is enough" was sure *NOT* "parity" with Caesar's armaments—and nowhere does he say, that I can find, "one sword is enough when Caesar reduces his stockpile to one sword, boys, and not before that!"

And if one sword, which be refused to use, was enough for Jesus, despite the number of swords Caesar had—then one nuclear warhead, which will not be used either—for first-strike, retaliatory strike, or any strike at all—will be enough for Christians as far as I am concerned, when I am running the Church!

\*　　\*　　\*

"Let him who is without sin cast the first stone," Jesus said—and no one threw a stone, not even Jesus. Does this mean that Jesus was not without sin—or does it mean that even he (she?) who is without sin doesn't throw stones either?

**REMEMBER** the blind man Jesus healed once, the one who said he couldn't tell if it was a man or a tree in the distance after he could see? And so then Jesus gave him another shot of healing and then the man saw clearly what was in the distance as well as what was up close. Well— perhaps the reason Paul saw "as through a glass darkly" is because Ananias did no better at healing his blindness than Jesus did on the first go-round for that blind man he had to heal twice—and Paul was so glad to see at all that he made no complaints as the other man did, and Ananias was so pleased that Paul could see after he laid his hands on him that he didn't check with Paul to see how well he could see (this was long before there were eye charts to read, etc.). Sometimes delight in just seeing keeps a person from demanding, often of him/her self, to see clearly—and so people go no further—desire no more, demand nothing but to see poorly as though through a glass darkly, figuratively speaking especially. Today no one would accept "seeing through a glass darkly" from an optometrist—but they will accept this in matters of mind or heart or faith, almost blindly.

Jesus had to heal the blind man twice before he had 20/20 vision, and perhaps Paul could have done with another shot of healing from Ananias so as to sing joyously, "I can see clearly now!" And not as through a glass darkly. And no doubt if he had met Jesus in person—had heard the Sermon on the Mount in person—there might be less of the "Pauline Theory" to try to make sense of, for Paul might have echoed the truth Jesus spoke and did, instead.

**Abbie Jane Wells**

**I WONDER** why the Church Fathers didn't dream up an Immaculate Conception for Joseph when they dreamed up one for Mary? I wonder if they thought something like that would have immunized Mary from the dangers of childbed fever when she gave birth in a cruddy stable as well as immunized her from sin, and left her pure and unsullied, untouched by the world or Joseph?

Surely Joseph, too, needed to be "set apart" from human feelings and sin and lust if he was to live under the same roof with Mary and serve as a pure and unsullied example of fatherhood, or step-fatherhood, to the Son—as pure and unsullied as the Church Fathers made Mary out to be.

I wonder if the Church Fathers think Joseph delivered Mary of Child with his eyes closed and with Mary's skirts primly down? Or don't they think this was as human a birth as any birth by woman is? Or don't they think, period?

**I THINK** the post-Christmas feelings of let-down and depression that many people have are like the "post-partum depression" that many people feel after giving birth. Now you've got that child that you so anxiously and excitedly waited for, and you are not sure you can handle it or all the changes it brings into your life—or if you will be able to cope with living with it on a day-to-day basis—24 hours every day, 7 days every week, 52 weeks every year—from now on.

**Abbie Jane Wells**

> "We celebrate Christ's first appearance at
> Christmas in order to anticipate with
> Unshakable Hope and Great Joy His Second
> Coming in Glory."
> *Words on a 1982 Christmas card*

**BUT IN** between his first coming and his second coming in Glory, there is an awful lot of living to be done on earth—and that requires living with the Babe born on Christmas day.

I celebrate Christmas because the world pregnant with the Christ has come full term and his time is upon us. And hopefully those who celebrate Christmas will let the Babe live—will not commit the infanticide of neglect by putting him back on the shelf until next Christmas—with an interim mourning of his crucifixion and celebration of his Easter resurrection, after which he is put back on the shelf—away from lives—until Christmas rolls around again.

No room in the Inn of Christian hearts and minds is a year-round happening for far too many. The Birth and the Child and the Man who grew from the Child are put aside—wrapped in every kind of padding, lest he come alive and take over our lives as any baby takes over the lives of those close.

After the anxiety and the dread as well as the excitement of the pregnancy of Advent comes the Birth—and after that is celebrated comes the postpartum depression; you've now got the child, now what are you going to do with it?

Well, there's a choice: commitment or neglect—let the child take over your lives or put him on a shelf—

63

away and separate—to be kept at a distance. "Don't let the gospel get within ten feet" is far too often the rule. Keep it and the Christ at a distance lest it, and he, grab you and change you and your way of living. No one wants a year-round Baby Jesus or grown-up Jesus any more than they want a year-round Christmas.

It was a woman, Mary, who first announced to the world, "He, the Christ, is conceived!"

And it was a woman, Mary, who ran to tell the disciples and the world, "He, the Christ, is risen!"

And might it not be that the Second Coming—still awaited—*did* take place "in *their* time," as the disciples and Paul expected—but that it wasn't recognized as such?

The First Coming: the empty womb of Mary.

The Second Coming; the empty tomb—and who's to say that he *didn't* come out of the tomb in a blaze of glory surrounded by heavenly hosts—nobody was there to see, all were hidden away in fear of maybe getting what he got on Good Friday if any one suspected they were his followers.

And is it not possible that his "Do not touch me. I have not yet gone to my Father" translates: "Don't touch me! I ain't dead yet! And I still have a man's feelings, woman!" to a woman that attracted him? Here he was—between the death MEN (not God) had done to him and leaving the earth permanently— caught between his deep and abiding love for the earth and all its people and going to his Father— pulled both ways equally, perhaps, during those days between Resurrection and Ascension; caught between the pull to stay with Mary, his mom and Joseph, and the earth's people whom he loved and the pull to go to his Father, whom he loved— caught between heaven and earth; perhaps not bound to either during those post-Resurrection days on earth, perhaps free to choose, who knows? One or the other but not both. "Don't touch me! I ain't dead yet!," for her touch might tip the balance toward staying rather than going to his Father—a temptation to stay with those he loved more than life itself? A temptation he would have to resist—the die had been cast by those who crucified, and yet he must have longed to stay with the earth's humanity he loved so dearly.

"Do not touch me. I have not yet gone to my Father," to me, contains all the human qualities and implications and longings of a living man who "ain't dead yet!"

**THIS** modern feminization of God, God as She rather than He, God as Mother rather than Father, may work some of the time, but it falls apart for me when I consider the conception of Jesus. The Mother God's seed? The Mother God and the woman Mary having a mutual Son? How could this be even with God to contrive it?

It takes two sexes to have a child of either sex—and I don't think two "she's" could do it even if one of them were God—not even with cloning rather than conception by Holy Spirit insemination. It takes one of each sex and with Mary the feminine, the Mother, for me that leaves it that God is the Father, the he—that is, if I am going to see Mary's Son Jesus as Son of God.

Now if God "created them in his Image, male and female he created them," I would assume there is as much of one of them in God as there is of the other—just as each of us is a 50/50 blend of mother and father, both male and female—though each of us is only one sex or the other.

Well, anyway, a Mother God and a Mother Mary would give Jesus two mothers and no father and, even if that were possible, it would remove him from being much of an example for all of us on earth with both mother and father. It would make him into something that human beings aren't and can't ever be, and what he could say and do or say for us to do would make no sense except to beings like him of which there are none on earth.

Women may not have liked having a father to boss them around, but let's face it, without our father's seed and heritage we wouldn't be at all. And women may not like a father God—but if they want the Christian heritage of Jesus: Son of Mary and Son of God—and with the mother Mary a known quantity and sex—the unknown who is the father of Jesus has to be the opposite—even in artificial insemination of Holy Spirit bearing the seed to Mary's womb.

Imagine Jesus calling Mary mother and also calling God mother—rather than "Two loves have I" as the old song goes, that would be "Two mothers have I" for him.

The fact that human men have misused their maleness—their likeness to a father God and a male Jesus—doesn't discredit what God himself is—it discredits the men who use this to lord it over women and to oppress women and to deny equality to women in church and state and business and marriage and in every other way they can. It is the men who need the changing in attitudes rather than God who needs a sex-change to give the women their rightful place in the world's scheme of things. It is the Church which needs the sex-change in attitudes rather than God who needs to have a "sex-change."

It is men and women together—50/50—who must live together and run the show in peace. As for the mother side of God and the father side—both of them are there in God even when he is called father—both are there in Jesus, and in all of us—both mother and father, regardless of whether we are male and female.

"... THE busyness of preparing the nursery ..." for Mary and Joseph was no "hanging the greens, the wreaths, the poinsettias." It was the mucking out of a cruddy stable so it would be as clean as possible for the birthing—and that would require some shoveling of manure out of the way, I would imagine, not the "hanging of greens, et al." Could it be that modern preparations in Churches as well as homes, the getting ready for Christmas, are "busyness for busyness sake," to keep you too busy to sit down and think about what "was born in a stable and laid in a manger" *really* involved for Mary and Joseph? We "Deck the halls with boughs of holly ..." and anything else we can think of—and never, or hardly ever think of the realities of the birth in a stable. We gussy up our churches with riches galore—and so distance ourselves from the home for the Christ Child that was the best that Joseph could provide, and very poor it was—to show how much fancier and richer a "home" *we* can provide in our gussied up churches and cathedrals—as if we were trying to shame Joseph—so fancy that street people wouldn't dare to wander in to a Christmas Eve service. Nor would the poor Mary and Joseph and Jesus, either!

"No room in the inn?" And churches often carry that on today: no room for the poor or the homeless or the street people at Christmas services or at any other time. Jesus in his three years of preaching and teaching *was* one of those we label as "street people"—"no place to lay his head," he said, a perfect description of street people. "No room in the inn." "No room in the churches"—what's the difference?

". . . The demands of church . . ." have become more and more oppressive—the "traditions" of Christmas, piled on top of each other—are as weighty for laity as for clergy—as weighty, at times, as the "weight of the Law" that Jesus did away with after a fashion. We add more and more—bury the gospel with our additions, and the "demands of the Church" leave little or no time for the demands of God or Jesus—for following the Ten Commandments, or the Sermon on the Mount, or Matthew 25: 35-40. Have we substituted the "demands of the Church" for the demands of God and Jesus? Have we made "the Church" our god? our idol?

"SANCTUARY for refugees" and "as you have done it to the least of these" takes on new meaning in the days following Christmas, as the fleeing from the slaughters in Central America—and the fleeing from the Slaughter of Innocents in Bethlehem for Mary and Joseph and the Babe—come together. And the deportations by Immigration Service, too, bear the load of that: "As you have done it to the least of these. . . ."

The refugees Mary and Joseph and the Babe—fleeing the bloodshed in Bethlehem before it happens to the Babe—going into a country that doesn't welcome them with open arms, either—unable to speak the language—Joseph needing a job; an illegal alien family from a disliked, if not hated, country—and from a despised people—and with, no doubt, no sanctuary waiting.This is being replayed in an increasing scale in our own country and all over the world, as the displaced by violence refugees seek sanctuary from bloodshed and death pour over borders.

No room in the inn of Bethlehem—no room in the country of Jesus' birth for sanctuary from despotic ruler and his soldiers—but they did somehow find room in a foreign country. Thank God Egypt had no Immigration Service in those days to hunt them down and deport them back into the life-threatening situation from which they had fled.

Both the churches which give sanctuary and the Immigration Service which denies it come under that "as you have done it to the least of these my brethren, you have done it unto me." One is counted among the sheep, on the right hand; and the other among the goats on the left—or rather, that is where *they* place themselves by their acts of mercy or acts of rejection and deportation.

And so it goes as the new year starts in the days after Christmas: people flee for their lives and the lives of their children, as Mary and Joseph fled for their lives and the life of Jesus—with no room in the inns of "the land of the free and the home of the brave," except for those few places where they can find sanctuary: may these increase to fill the need—and SOON.

And in our streets are homeless people: home-grown "refugees" from our own economic distress and disasters, and they are termed "street people," often in derogatory fashion. "Why don't they get a job?" is said of the jobless in a time of high unemployment because there are no jobs to be had. "Why doesn't the private sector take care of them?" is said by government as it slashes humanitarian programs in order to beef up the already gross and bloated military.

We forget that Jesus left a good job as a carpenter to "go off on a wild goose chase," as I am sure must have been said of him by many of his contemporaries—to become a street person doing a street ministry—a "refugee" from the market-place job, so again "as you have done it to the least of these" street people, as well as refugees, comes alive in our midst, for Jesus was one of "them" in both instances, sure as shooting.

**CHRISTMAS ONE** is over in Bethlehem, and life goes on. As usual? Well, not hardly. The shepherds have gone back to their flocks, 'tis true—and the wise men have gone, by the back way, back to where they came from—and Mary and Joseph and the Babe have taken off in a hurry for Egypt. But in Bethlehem the days of mourning the slaughtered babes still goes on—and the clean-up of blood—and the dealing with griefs and angers and frustrations.

Christmas One is over and life goes on for Mary and Joseph and the Babe. As usual? Well, not hardly. A quick, unplanned trip as political refugees has nothing of "the usual" about it. It isn't a vacation trip south—or north—if you are refugees with a price on the head of any one of you. There is the daily grind of finding food and making camp, a "secure" camp hidden from those who might be chasing you hoping to catch you. There is the daily grind of putting as many miles as possible between you and "them"—and when there is a Babe, that adds to the anxiety.

Christmas 1984 is over—and life goes on. As usual? Yep, pretty much. Everybody goes back to the "normal" life—some take trips of R & R, to recover from the rigors of the Christmas season. "We really did it up brown this year but, my, it *was* tiring"—so it's time for a trip for R & R—a trip *not* like the trip Mary and Joseph took after Christmas One—Oh, Dear Lord, no—not like *that*.

Christmas 1984 is over and there is little mourning for the babes slaughtered in Bethlehem so long ago— except for a few odd-balls, by the world's and the

**Abbie Jane Wells**

Church's standards, who mourn the deaths in witness at the Pentagon, as they work to prevent future
nuclear slaughters of babes, as well as men and
women.

**CHRISTMAS 1984** is over, and life goes on as usual, in Church and out—while Mary and Joseph and the Babe shlep their way to Egypt's refugee sanctuary—as forgotten in churches as out, now that the Big Bash Christmas has become is over and done with. The trip to Egypt, too, is part of the Christmas story, but you'd never know it. Church school children *are* told a bit about Mary and Joseph's trip *from* Nazareth *to* Bethlehem, but not much is said about their trip *from* Bethlehem to Egypt. Nor do adults, laity, dwell too much on the months, maybe even years, *after* Christmas and what they must have been like for Mary and Joseph, alone with the Babe, in a foreign country. "As soon as Mary delivers the baby," she and Joseph are dropped, you might say, from Church thinking or anybody's thinking—as are the refugees pouring from country to country in our world today. Jesus wasn't woofing when he said "As you did it to the least of these you did it unto me," except he could have added, "for you have done it to me *first*." As our treatment of modern day refugees as well as our treatment of the Refugee Holy Family clearly shows.

There is a telling commentary in *Newsweek's* "Never Again, Until Tomorrow" (Jan. 3, 1983, p. 57):

> "There is a myth, spread by preachers and their near cousins, editorial writers, that the function of the holidays is to remind us to be virtuous all year long, while in fact their purpose is to concentrate all our virtuous activity into a couple of days, so we can safely forego it the rest of the year. . . ."

**Abbie Jane Wells**

And so it is—we concentrate Christmas into the birth of the Christ Child and then drop it and forget the rest of the story that comes attached—as we go our usual way after Christmas and take our vacation trips to recuperate from our excesses—whether secular or religious—of doing Christmas up brown— while Mary and Joseph and the Christ Child shlep it to Egypt alone with hardly a thought from us who were so ecstatic about the Birth . . . the birth, yes but not that trip as refugees to Egypt and in Egypt. *That* part of the Christmas story we are ready to skip entirely—in our living as well as in our thinking. It's "Never Again, Until Next Christmas," and then we will think again about the Birth of the Christ Child—but little about the nine months of the Christ Child in utero of the pregnancy for Mary, and Joseph, too—or the months after Christmas, or even years, of their lives as political refugees in a country that doesn't exactly welcome them with open arms; nor do the people, we would imagine. We distance ourselves from that part of the Christmas story—or that sequel to the Christmas story, as if it were the plague. We distance ourselves from what Joseph did daily for the Christ Child, before as well as after Birth, and concentrate instead on the gifts the wise men brought and the awe and adoration of them and the shepherds, and the angels singing—all of whom made a one-time appearance and then disappeared from the scene and from the life of the Christ Child. While it was Joseph who stayed and did daily all that needed to be done for the Christ Child and his Mother. The dailiness of Joseph—no time off for good behavior—no R & R trips—is the prime example of discipleship—and we distance ourselves from Joseph's example in every which way we can, lest we be tempted to "go, thou, and do likewise."

We wait for a "sign" before we act on behalf of others—but rarely do we wait for a "sign" when we plan our own pleasures. Pentagon spending is seen as a "theft from the poor"—but rarely is our spending for our own excesses and pleasures seen in this light.

And so it goes after this Christmas, as after every Christmas. Except for Joseph, who, after the rigors of Christmas One, took Mother and Child to Egypt without taking a vacation first to rest up after all he had been put through to get the "Christmas Christ Child" show on the road! Joseph could probably have used a week off then—or if not then, surely *after* the trip to Egypt was completed. Mary, too, could have done with a bit of R & R after the birthing as well as after that rigorous, to say the least, trip to Egypt. A week at an Egyptian health spa, or resort, would have done Mary and Joseph, and the Babe, too, a world of good! They would have come away refreshed for the duties ahead.

Well, I doubt if they ever got a day-off from Bethlehem on—no "annual leave"—no "sick leave," either—no "vacation with pay."

This Christmas is over and the Holy Family, literally as well as figuratively, is wrapped in cotton and stored away with the Christmas tree ornaments and other do-dads, to be thought of "Never Again until Next Christmas."

And so it goes. . . .

**Abbie Jane Wells**

**COULD** Mary have kept a kosher home in Egypt? cooked kosher? And what if she could not? Throughout history Jews have starved to death rather than eat non-kosher food—their children, too; but this was a luxury Mary and Joseph could hardly afford—for the child was the Son of God as well as of Mary, and it was their job to keep him alive for God and the world—and themselves, too, so they could care for him.

So what to do when there was only non-kosher food available—no kosher sections in the Egyptian markets—and there must have been times when non-kosher food was all they could get, or afford. There must have been some serious discussions between Mary and Joseph and some after the son was old enough to understand—and precocious as he must have been, he would have understood early. And there must have been some agonizing and breast-beating when there was nothing but forbidden food available which the son would have to eat if he was to eat and grow. And this may have laid the groundwork for Jesus' seeming indifference to strict kosher laws when he was a man. He had seen in his own home what trying to live up to them could do to people, when he was small and living in Egypt.

On the trip from Bethlehem to Egypt it must have gotten harder and harder to find kosher food—and when they crossed the border into Egypt it must have gotten damn near impossible. Food was bound to have been on their mind almost constantly on that trip and while in Egypt—and doubly so: food—and food that wasn't forbidden.

How could you even occasionally feed the son forbidden food and at the same time teach that Jews couldn't eat this? Well—that must have weighed heavy on Mary and Joseph—and all this Jesus would store in his memory to think about, and later to speak out about.

And if Joseph was forced to work on the Sabbath because Egyptian employers paid no attention to any Sabbath, much less the Jewish Sabbath; that, too, must have gone hard with Joseph—he had to work if he were to be able to feed the son, and in order to work he may have had to desecrate the Sabbath and Jesus must have heard Joseph's anguish and felt the tension in the household and started thinking along lines that would later become his, "The Sabbath was made for man, not man for the Sabbath" which caused him some censure and trouble from the orthodox authorities.

To be a Jew in Egypt in the first century—to start to raise the son a Jew in Egypt—must have meant many crises of conscience. Trying to keep all the religious laws in a country that kept none of them—and without a community of faith, or a rabbi, like in Israel, to give them advice and support; to have to make every decision that involved the practice of religion by yourselves, without any guidance, that must have been Mary's and Joseph's lot while in Egypt. Life was sure no picnic for Mary and Joseph while they were in Egypt—religiously or in any other way—and that's for sure.

**Abbie Jane Wells**

**SAYING** "God's becoming Man," to describe the Incarnation, makes as much sense to me as saying the Incarnation was "Mary's becoming Man." Men—and women, too—tend to forget that Jesus was as much the son of Mary's humanity as he was the son of God's Divinity.

And saying, "Mary, mother of God," makes about as much sense to me as saying, "Abbie, mother of Eddie" to show the parenthood of our son Brian.

And God as "She" doesn't make any sense to me at all—that would make Jesus the son of not one mother, but two! And even with a little genetic engineering by God himself (herself?) I don't think that's a possibility.

Trying to make the son of God into something he isn't won't work. Whatever God had in mind for his son to be—God was limited by Mary's humanity—if one wants to use the word "limited" in reference to any human, even Mary—or especially Mary. The size of the son was limited to the size of Mary's womb—not by the size of God's dreams and hopes for his son! Mary's womb would only stretch so far without bursting at the seams—so God's son *had* to be human-sized, regardless of how much men would like to make him God-size.

Jesus was a 50/50 blend of mother and father—like all men and women—and he was as much of his mother, though male, as he was of his Father—like all men are. And not all that he preached and taught was only learned "from his Father in heaven." Some of it he learned from his mother—and some he learned from Joseph—and some he learned all by himself or from others. And who is to say which is which.

Jesus was—and is—a "half-breed"—half human and half divine—all mixed together inseparably—the "two flesh made one and let no man (or woman) put asunder."

Jesus was as much son of Mary (son of Man) as he was son of God—and I wish men—and women—would quit leaving Mary out of the mix—and out of the picture! Jesus was 50 percent God—God "watered down" with 50 percent of Mary's humanity! He had to be regardless of how much many wish he wasn't.

**THE DOWNWARD MOBILITY** of Mary and Joseph: from home and job or business in Nazareth—to a stable or cave in Bethlehem—to a time on the lam through the desert with little but the clothes on their backs and a new-born Babe—into Egypt to live as refugees—is rarely thought of in good times or bad. But now with the plight of refugees and the homeless and unemployed or under-employed on a world-wide basis as well as in the U.S. being reported in media of every description, it is hard to continue to overlook this fact.

Joseph especially must have felt like the rug had been pulled out from under him for sure as they took their journey down, down, down the economic ladder to just about rock-bottom in Egypt as fairly illegal aliens, besides being political refugees, in a land that was unfriendly and whose language they didn't speak.

Sanctuary? I doubt that there was any sanctuary of supportive people waiting for them in Egypt.

Housing? There wasn't any housing waiting for them in Egypt any more than there had been in Bethlehem—nothing available that was comparable to what they had in Nazareth, poor though that may have been. And until Joseph could get the wise men's gift of gold changed into coin of the realm—and with no proof of ownership, this "exchange" would come with a hefty discount attached—Joseph and Mary would have been really hard up to find housing as soon as they arrived. Well—Joseph and Mary had some gold—and nobody, but nobody, dealing in gold in Egypt was likely to believe any story about three wise men riding in from the East and dumping not only gold but frankincense and myrrh into the Babe's lap! Besides, Joseph had to be careful who he let in on the secret for fear they would be robbed after the gold was exchanged if not before. Exchanging or selling the wise men's gifts would tide them over, no doubt, until Joseph found work.

So here is this poor young couple chosen by God to be the mother and step-father of his son on earth—thousands of miles from home and family—in the situation of being worse off than they had been in Nazareth when they each said their "Yes" to God. Starting out pretty much from scratch—starting over again—in a foreign land that wasn't friendly nor were its people—who no doubt still bore a grudge against the slaves, the Israelites, and their descendants, who had walked out on their Egyptian overlords and left all the shit-work behind for the Egyptian poor to do. A grudge can be held for centuries and frequently is—especially against a people who freed themselves from domination on their own initiative or on God's initiative and help—as Mary and Joseph may well have found out. Seeking sanctuary in a country your ancestors fled from? Well, that isn't the best place to seek sanctuary, but evidently that was the best place for Mary and Joseph to go in God's opinion, a safer place for them, evidently, than their own country was.

But can't you just see Joseph asking for a job from some Egyptian carpenter or builder, after he learned

**Abbie Jane Wells**

enough of the language to be able to follow directions and specifications, to get: "You, an Israelite, want me to give you a job? No way! You people can't be depended on not to walk off the job and leave it unfinished."

**SPEAKING** of holding grudges, I wonder how many of the crowd crying "Crucify! Crucify!", some thirty years and more later, had been nursing a grudge ever since the slaughter of babes in Bethlehem—a grudge against the Babe who "got away" rather than against Herod and his soldiers? Or were there some leftovers from Herod's soldiers or court who had spent their years since Bethlehem hoping some day to be able to do for the dead Herod what he hadn't been able to do for himself while he was alive: get that Stable Babe out of the way, whatever his age, no matter how long it took? Were there still people who had been involved in the Bethlehem massacre, or bereaved by it, who had sworn, if only to themselves, to finish the job—or to help and approve, what Herod's soldiers weren't able to accomplish—who wanted to get rid of the one they thought caused the massacre at Bethlehem, who blamed the Stable Babe rather than Herod for the massacre. Grieving parents of children who have been killed in acts of violence can hold grudges for years, even generations, waiting for a chance to "get even"—as history shows clearly.

**WELL,** to get back to Mary and Joseph in Egypt, no matter how poor a house or business they had left in Nazareth, it must have seemed wonderful in retrospect compared with what they ended up with in Egypt. "Not to worry. God will provide" didn't seem to pay off in any material way for them or their son, according to gospel accounts, and I doubt that it did during their time in Egypt, either. They had a bit to tide them over, when or if they were able to exchange or sell the wise men's gifts—but that wouldn't last long—no "savings account" does and this couldn't be drawn on forever. Like any unemployed, Joseph, an alien, maybe even an illegal alien, had to find work of some kind, no doubt at less than minimum wages for Egyptians (there may have been an "Egyptian jobs for Egyptians" policy!)—and Mary had to make do on whatever Joseph could provide.

But what a come down this must have been compared with Nazareth. Because they each had said "Yes" to God's requests of them, they ended up, at least for awhile, much worse off than they had ever been in their life! What a strain this must have been on their faith; their faith in themselves as well as in God. Joseph had to believe in his abilities even when he couldn't find work all the time, even when the pay for what work he did was sub-standard pay—and Mary had to believe in him—and both had to keep their faith in humanity as well as in God, no matter what, as well as keep God's son alive and well.

Their lives tend to disprove, I think, any "If you only *believe*, all will be well," that gets tossed around lightly by those who preach what I think are false "truths" about God as well as humanity, as they lead the rousing singing of the old Hymn:"God will take care of you through every day in every way. . . ."

The world is full of people today in situations comparable to that of Mary and Joseph in Egypt, or worse, believers as well as non-believers, whether they are refugees, or aliens, or citizens—for Mary's and Joseph's and the Babe's life in Egypt was probably no different, except for their faith in God, than that of the poor or destitute Egyptian.

And so it goes—today as always—and it sure as hell *shouldn't.*

**Abbie Jane Wells**

**"THE POOR** you will always have *with* you"—one of the reasons being that most usually they can't afford the cost of moving somewhere else—or do not have the physical energy to. For the "poor" includes the destitute, the malnourished, as well as those who have barely enough. Somewhere else there might be work, they might have a chance to better themselves, to "make it," if only barely. But there are costs to moving which the poor often can't meet, and so: "the poor you will always have with *you*" as they cannot afford to move away from *you*.

**WHAT** the story of Jesus and the Syro-Phoenician woman says to me is more about Jesus than the woman—and here I would connect that Scripture with the one about the wedding at Cana. In both instances Jesus was not above listening to what a woman had to say—and changing his mind and actions because of what a woman said.

He did the miracle of removing the evil spirit from the woman's daughter in the first instance. And he turned water into wine (or added "spirits") in the second—and both because a woman told him something different than what he had on his mind to do— or not do, proving that Jesus had an "open readiness"—a willingness, fairly total, to listen to human beings, even women yet, as well as to God! He changed his attitude as well as his mind at least two different times because two different women spoke up; called his attention to something he had missed seeing.

And remember, it was not the woman who referred to "one does not give to dogs" first, it was Jesus—but her shooting back at him "but even the dogs get the crumbs . . ." wasn't exactly groveling. Jesus is lucky she didn't bite or claw him!

Jesus' healing the woman's daughter after their exchange of words wasn't exactly "crumbs under the table" but the full measure of healing the Jewish "children" got. And I'll bet Jesus never even implied again that a non-Jew—man, woman or child—was "a dog." Jesus treated the Syro-Phoenician woman and her daughter as equal in stature to Jews without making her change or convert into one first. That is, he did *after* she stood up to him and spoke her piece, and in those days that took more guts than humility, believe you me!

A third instance in the New Testament of a woman speaking up is the story Jesus told about the woman who kept hammering away at the judge who kept ignoring her "beef" until she literally wore him down and he took care of her "beef," "lest she drive me to distraction," or words to that effect. Didn't Jesus cite this as an example of how persistence pays off? It sure isn't any example of a woman "growing smaller in her own right" or "humbling herself." I see this as an example of a person—man or woman—becoming bigger and gutsier, daring to speak up, and out, to an authority figure.

It could well be said of the episode between Jesus and the Syro-Phoenician woman: "It was a learning experience for Jesus."

**IN 1973** I heard a woman in her seventies, and wise, say "only a woman could have the Son for God, and I don't think the men will ever forgive us for that."

By the same token, God and Mary had a son, whether by Godly design or by the happenstance of human birth is debatable perhaps, but it may be that women, or some of them, will never forgive God for that.

We each are both male and female 50/50—whatever our sex, by virtue of having a parent of each sex—but the Biblical writers and Biblical people didn't know this and so to them men were all male and women were all female—and God, being father, was all male rather than any 50/50 blend of the masculine and feminine. The Scriptures say, "In his Image he made them—male and female he made them," and no doubt Adam and Eve, each in their own right and sex, were both this male and female blend by virtue of this.

The fact that men have used this 100 percent male concept, both for God and themselves and for Jesus, has been aided and abetted in days gone by by women who didn't know any better either.

But now we know a lot more about the reproduction process and genetics than has ever been known before—and we continue to learn more and more and so concepts about men and women as well as about God and Jesus are changing. But old concepts die hard, die a lingering death, and until we each see ourselves as both male and female, as much one as the other, regardless of sex, we won't be able to imagine God as both masculine and feminine regardless of whatever human pronoun is used to address him/her.

Perhaps this is one of the reasons the early religious Jews and some still today would not say the name of God, because it tends to label and sexualize the One who is unknowable.

Recently I heard a naive young woman—religiously trained, too, a nun—say she sometimes thought maybe Jesus chose men to be his disciples to make up to men for the fact that God chose a woman to bear the Son—as if God had a choice in the matter! As if it were an "eenie, meenie, minie, mo" decision between choosing man or woman to bear the Son— and since God "chose" woman, then Jesus chose men to be disciples as a sort of consolation prize for me! I think that's about as far-fetched as one can get! And in this day and age, too!

It may take a generation or more of gradually adapting our minds to the fact that both men and women are a blend of both masculine and feminine traits rather than only one or the other, before men are comfortable with having feminine as well as masculine traits and women are comfortable with having masculine as well as feminine traits—or adapting to seeing the feminine and mothering half of a masculine and fathering God.

Though children may "take after" one parent or the other, they remain a 50/50 blend of both parents, inseparable and indivisible—and if we all are images of the creator God—then God is this same blend— inseparable and indivisible.

But it will take some time for this to soak into people who have thought otherwise since thinking began—since The Bible was written—since Judaism and then Christianity were born of human minds and hearts.

Sexist language in the Bible has to be taken with a grain of salt, remembering that the writers and the people didn't know anything else in those days. But we do now, and we can't interpret Scripture through sexist eyes any longer, lest we perpetuate the myths this promotes in churches and out.

**Abbie Jane Wells**

**I WONDER** how many went out to hear Jesus at the well because of the Samaritan woman's "He told me all that I have ever done," thinking "Wow, *that* ought to be good"? Nudging each other and giving knowing glances, as if her saying that was like a "come on" on a theater marquee: "See! Hear! *All* she has ever done!" which packs 'em in—or like a "bares all" book promotion.

How many went out to hear Jesus thinking *this* was what they would get to hear—that Jesus would tell *them* this part of what he had told the Samaritan woman? Knowing men and women, I imagine they were much the same in Jesus' day as in our day—and an "expose" of sexual conduct would probably have drawn a crowd then as now—even the suggestion of such, even where one was *not* intended, would be enough to cause many people to go to hear someone they *thought* was going to fill them in on some titillating details.

Little did they know that this *wasn't* what they would hear when they went to the well to hear the man the Samaritan woman told them about. Of course, not everyone who went to hear Jesus thought they would get to hear some juicy tidbits about the woman, but I'll bet more did than we would like to think did.

Instead, Jesus no doubt turned the tables on them, and pointed out to them all that *they*, not the woman, had done, making them think about all *they* had ever done, as well as heavenly things.

**I WONDER** which of the men whose bills the wily steward discounted behind the boss's back could be counted on to give him a job when he got fired for this, knowing what he did when the boss's back was turned.

The "Master commended the dishonest steward for his prudence." And I wondered if that wasn't said with a bit of sarcasm attached? And could Jesus' "make friends for yourself by means of unrighteous mammon so that when it fails you they may receive you . . ." were pure, unadulterated sarcasm? Were the men whom the steward discounted likely to "receive him" into their household as steward?

Wow! Did that wily steward ever get fooled! I'll bet there wasn't one of those men so willing to be on the receiving end of his discounts who would have wanted him in his own household working as steward, or anything else. I doubt if any of those "discounted" men would have been so foolish as to hire that "wily"(?) steward so he could discount *their* customer behind their backs. That "wily"(?) steward's "prudence" sure shot hell out of any chance he might have had of getting a job as steward with any of the men he discounted—or with anyone else in the area, either. For the boss, as well as the discounted men, would surely spread the word around that this steward was dishonest and couldn't be trusted. I doubt very much that the discounted men as well as the boss were likely to give him a "good recommendation" to another employer. The wily steward, I would say, really cooked his own goose in this, that's for sure!

**Abbie Jane Wells**

We hear sermons all the time about the wily steward and what he did—but rarely, if ever, does anyone preach a sermon about the men who took the discounts he handed out: his willing accomplices. What about them and what *they* did that cut into the wily steward's boss's rightful profits? In this day and age with corporate under-the-counter deals and bribes in the news, it may be time for some sermons about the men who helped the steward to be wily—about those who received as well as the one who gave the discounts—those who assisted him—and the morality of what *they* did behind the boss's back and at the boss's expense. *They* were the ones who profited, not the "wily"(?) steward—and their part in this under-the-counter, behind the boss's back deal just may fit the situations modern men and women get caught up in today a lot more than what the wily steward did ever does. We all are a lot more likely to take the discounts offered us, without question, than we are likely to offer unauthorized discounts to further our own position—or are we? Both the wily steward *and* his willing accomplices are suspect.

**'TIS TRUE:** "Finally Jesus warned us that there would be wars until he comes again. . . ." But in my Bible, he says, "You will HEAR of war and rumors of war . . ." NOT: you will *participate* in wars and *pay* for wars and *pay* for the preparations for war, ad infinitem (and ad nauseum).

And Bishop Kenny of Juneau sums it up beautifully with his: "For us as Christians, the basic issue remains not what an enemy may or may not do, but what we as the followers of Jesus must or must not do."

And I say "Amen" to that—

So let's get the lead out!

**Abbie Jane Wells**

IF "In the cross is our salvation"—if the Crucifixion is in God's plan for salvation, redemption, etc., then why do we label those who "assisted" God in carrying this "plan" to fruition as "all the scheming, plotting, grasping of the ugly slippery characters whose names are forever blackened by Good Friday's event?"

If we say "the end never justifies the means" for using violence against people or a person (in a "good" cause) why do we act as if "salvation and redemption" justifies the crucifixion? That the crucifixion is a justifiable means for *God* to use for *his* purposes, that is, but not for humans to use.

If God OKed his son's crucifixion as a means for "paradise regained" for us, would he then say "and a pox on you, may your names be forever blackened" of those who did the crucifixion, evidently, "for" him?

If "in the cross is our salvation" is true, should not the ones who took part in it and thereby set into motion that "cross is our salvation" be called saints rather than blackguards?

Can anyone, even God, use a bad and cruel and violent means: crucifixion, to achieve a good end: salvation, redemption, etc.; i.e. would a good God use a cruel means?

Can anyone, under the "Thou shalt not kill" Commandment, even God, use violence and killing, either to accomplish the crucifixion, or to try to stop it once it was set into motion by men? The only non-violent way to stop the crucifixion—or any death penalty—is for the judges to reverse their decision, or for the ruler to commute the sentence. And those who could have stopped the crucifixion nonviolently—Pilate, Herod, etc., didn't.

And if God, "like any good father on earth," as Jesus once said, is bound by the same rules and regs and commandments he hands down to his children, God couldn't stop the crucifixion by killing the crucifiers and soldiers, no matter how badly he wanted to—for God, too, is bound by that "Thou shalt not kill," even to save his own son. And it would have been unseemly, to say the least, for the Father God to use violence and killing to save the life of his non-violent son who had renounced the use of all violence and killing.

Humanity's cry of "why would a good God allow the crucifixion of his son if he wasn't in on it or didn't OK it?" was echoed in recent history with "How could a good God allow the Holocaust to happen?"

Mostly, I would say, because a "good God" doesn't use violence even for a good end; like stopping his son's crucifixion—or stopping the horrors of the Holocaust.

It is up to the *people* who set these horrors into motion to reverse their decisions and actions—and when they don't, God doesn't step in and do it for them—and that *doesn't* mean that he condones their acts of violence or has some ulterior—or even superior—reason of his own for "allowing" the horror to happen, or continue, or that it's "his will," either.

Jesus' "My God, My God, why have you forsaken me?" has been echoed and re-echoed by countless

**Abbie Jane Wells**

thousands—millions—Jews and others in concentration camps, going to gas chambers, etc., and by the survivors, and by the families and friends. And from religious people throughout the world came, "How could a good God allow the Holocaust to happen?"

To me, the Holocaust is the crucifixion multiplied six million times, and more. "How could a good God allow such horrors to happen?" *Why* would he "allow" such horrors to happen? For "salvation"? For "redemption"? Well, I doubt that very much.

Rather than "How could a good God allow such horrors to happen?" it is "How could good religious people allow such horrors to happen—be a party to such horrors?" And the answer to that is as varied as the people who stand by and do nothing to stop it, or who "obey orders" and participate in the horrors, or who remain silent or join in with the mobs who cry, "Crucify! Crucify!" or any other "final solution"— and then in the aftermath, label those as animals or barbarians whose acts they had applauded, or silently watched.

"Were you there when they crucified our Lord?" Doing nothing but watching and weeping? Hidden away in fear? Applauding the court's decision? Applauding those who carried out the court's orders?

Did you lose faith in a God who did nothing to stop his son's crucifixion? Did you lose faith in a God who "allowed" the Holocaust to happen? Or did you, rather, think that God, too, is as bound to nonviolence as was his son, because "Thou shalt not kill" is as binding on the law giver as it is on the law receiver? Even when it is God—*especially* when it is God?"

**WHEN** I am Pope, if I declare a Holy Year, it will be a Holy Year of acts of mercy based on Matthew: 34-36, etc., with a morotorium on pilgrimages to Rome or anywhere else—the pilgrimage expense money being spent instead for feeding the hungry, clothing the naked, housing the homeless, etc. And Lord knows, the world is full of them everywhere you look. Money spent on pilgrimages while there are hungry and starving people in the world to be fed and homeless people in the world needing a roof over their head, is as much a "theft from the poor" as money spent on nuclear arms and munitions ever is.

No wonder Jesus said "The poor you will always have with you!" He knew full well, I am sure, that money would be spent gussying up religion, "in his name" before money was spent on acts of mercy to lift the poor out of their poverty, so there would always be people whose basic needs were not being met—as much "thanks" to religious people's neglect as Caesar's.

When people heed the Pope's call to shlep it to Rome on pilgrimage, what happens to Jesus' call to feed the hungry, clothe the naked, house the homeless, etc., in a world where 30 children die of starvation every 60 seconds? How many more children will die and how many more go unfed during the Pope's Holy Year because the money is spent on pilgrimages rather than on the glaring needs of the poor of the world?

Does not one accrue a debt to the poor at least equal to what is spent on our Churchy get-togethers-conventions, reunions, as well as pilgrimages, etc.?

**Abbie Jane Wells**

Does anyone ever think of spending, say $3,500, on the needs of the world's poor *instead* of making a pilgrimage, or *in addition to* making a pilgrimage? If "Thou shalt love thy neighbor as thyself," should not one spend as much on "thy neighbors" needs as on thyself's in-house religious extras?

Are those who remain at home to be asked to pray that the hungry won't starve to death while money is being spent by others for "spiritual experiences" as well as a little sightseeing?

In the 20th century, Jesus' "I was hungry and you fed me not," might be followed by "you went on pilgrimage to Rome instead" or on any of the other things people spend money on in the name of religion which leaves little or no money left over to meet the needs of the world's hungry and starving and homeless and naked or underclothed.

For people so concerned for full-term life for all fetuses, there seems to be little concern for the life after birth of those fetuses in a world where 30 children starve to death every 60 seconds while "business as usual" goes on apace in Church as well as State.

**AS FOR** the why of Jesus' reason for waiting 30 years to begin his public ministry? I would assume it was because it took him that long to practice out in the world's market-place what he would later preach; to experience himself as well as observe Mary's and Joseph's and other's experience, especially the poor, to meet the world's temptations face-to-face, for the three temptations in the desert weren't the only temptations he had to say "no thanks" to. He practiced it all *before* he preached it. And this took him until age 30.

And when I am Pope, the candidates for ordination will have to go out into the world's marketplace after seminary graduation to practice what they have learned, to try it on for size—and then when they are 30, after their years of applying the things they were taught in seminary (or trying to) out in the world's marketplace, then will come ordination, if they still desire it and feel up to preaching what they have learned while practicing theological truths in the world, devoid of "religious" titles or status.

Not only did Jesus live what he would later preach *after* he had lived it and tested it, and himself; he watched Mary and Joseph live it, too, so he knew it could be done by ordinary human beings as well as himself. And Mary and Joseph must have measured up, for nowhere is it written that anyone ever threw up to Jesus how poorly Mary and Joseph practiced what he preached! No record of anyone saying, "Why don't you tell *that* to your old man? Joseph isn't doing so hot, either," when Jesus was laying it on the line! And that's about the first thing people do when you are telling them how they should live; they either throw up to you how poorly your parents are practicing what you are preaching, or how lousy your kids are doing it, when they can't accuse you yourself of poor practice of your own preaching.

Jesus practiced it for 30 years before he felt ready to go out and preach it to others besides family—and he practiced it out in the world's marketplace where everyone else has to practice it; earning his living by the sweat of his brow and the work of his hands just like everybody else, with no more "subsidy" from God or Temple or Caesar than anyone else got. No wonder "He knew what he was about!" He had learned from his own experience and the experience of others, not from abstract theological theories found only in books or lectures from "professional" religionists. He had *lived* it before he tried to preach it to others. And it could very well be that until this was accomplished there would be no—could be no "The Spirit of the Lord is upon me, he has annointed me . . ." for him—or any other preacher-teacher, either.

**IF YOU** re-cast the Good Samaritan story into today's world, into the Church scene in U.S. of A., it would be a Christian "Levite" and priest who scurried on by—on their way to church perhaps, maybe even to a discussion on non-Christian people or regimes.

It was the good and pious people of Jesus' day, those who may have never missed a scheduled Temple service, who passed the robbed and beaten man by—and it was the man despised by them and their religion, the Samaritan who stopped and took care of him—the Samaritan who would *not* have been welcome on Temple property even as a visitor.

So today we would have the good and pious Christians—on the way perhaps to church service or maybe a discussion on unGodly Communism and the dastardly Soviets and what was wrong with them—passing the robbed and beaten on the world's highways and byways—and perhaps the "good Samaritan" today might be a good communist or some Christian who wasn't known to be a gung-ho "anticommunist" fanatic, or a supporter of some Christian body like UCC or WCC or the Quakers, etc., who give aid to all sides, all ideologies, when the need arises.

And there is the possibility that the robbed and beaten man himself was a Samaritan—or communist in today's world—and then it would be no wonder that the pious and self-righteous "religious" people passed on by so as not to "give aid and comfort" to "the enemy." They wouldn't touch a robbed and beaten "enemy" with a 10 foot pole even if he (or she) would die otherwise. They were too "religious" to soil themselves or their reputations by giving aid to someone whom they considered heathen, or atheist, or anti whatever they themselves were.

And so today, no aid should be given to anyone not Christian and American oriented—that's giving aid to the "enemy," or supporting violence to over-zealous critics of UCC and WCC—one can only be a "good Samaritan" to those who support our own religion and nation, or else you are a "supporter" and booster of suspect ideologies and strange religions or no religion at all.

I wonder how many discussions were sparked in Temple circles between priests and Levites and any-one else who could get a word in edgewise—after Jesus' telling the Good Samaritan parable—on "what is wrong with Samaritans?" and "what is wrong with Samaritan-ism?" You can be sure this parable didn't spark many debates in Temple circles on "What is wrong with priests and Levites who do not stop to help the robbed and beaten on the Jerico Road?" (Or any other road, either!)

The parable doesn't say who the robbed and beaten man was—what his ideology or religion was—he could have been a revolutionary, a Zealot or a Roman, even, as well as a Jew or Samaritan or Greek. He bears no "label" in Jesus' parable—nor status symbol of any kind—he could have been any of the "undesirables" of that day—or of this day, and of all the years in between. He could have been any of those labeled "undesirable" or "heretic" or "enemy" by religion or Church or State, even an "illegal alien"—or legal "alien"—anyone judged "off limits" by religions and nations, Christian and otherwise.

And here some words of Daniel Berrigan come to mind:

". . . In any real understanding there aren't any Russians anymore and there aren't any Americans—there are human beings in a leaking scow. And I refuse to look to the right or left of me to see if it's a yellow face on a black face or a Russian face. I want to see some people bailing and I want to see some people rowing because there are children in this lousy boat and we are in deep trouble—and we'd better start asserting a common humanity and a common danger and stop talking about Russians."

And I say "Amen" to that.

**Abbie Jane Wells**

# THE HOLY SPIRIT

> "... And I believe in the Holy Ghost, the Lord and Giver of Life, who proceedeth from the Father ..."

The Holy Ghost, impregnator of Mary physically—with seed of God in a holy artificial insemination—and "when his time had come" the son bursts forth from the womb of Mary—*not* full-grown, but a tiny babe to grow and mature, and grow in wisdom in the world.

And might this not be a physical analogy to what happens spiritually to everyone who says a total "yes" to God as Mary did—God's Holy Spirit impregnates them spiritually with a minute seed of God's Spirit, his essence—which if we don't abort it accidently or on purpose by qualifying or renouncing our "yes," grows within us until its time is come upon us and it in us bursts forth in a way that changes our lives, as we change with it, as it grows and matures, and each of us along with it—and we grow in wisdom along with it?

The Incarnation in Mary—of Mary—being a physical and visible showing of the spiritual and invisible incarnation within each one who is willing, ready or not, men and women alike, for the Holy Spirit to plant the seed of God within them—making them pregnant with God, by God, on a full-time basis, as any physical pregnancy is a full time thing, and is an experience of growth and enlargement within—so it is also with a spiritual pregnancy.

"The Holy Spirit is a feeling of an unseen third person," someone wrote me once. And I thought, "a third person of many moods, no doubt—now raging at us for our apathy and slowness to comprehend—now a comforting presence during our sorrows and disappointments and times of loneliness—now a prodder trying to light a fire beneath us, or within us—what ever we *really* need at a specific time, but not always what *we think* we need at a particular time. Sets us afire when we need to be—calms us down, dampens our angers, when our "fire" burns too hot and threatens to devour us and/or others.

**Abbie Jane Wells**

**CONSIDER** Joseph—stuck in Nazareth after Jesus took off on his preaching-teaching journeys—after Mary took off and went with him, too.

Consider the looks and remarks Joseph probably got when Jesus didn't come back for visits, to check on how things were going for his father, Joseph—nor is there any record of Mary returning for any visits, either. I wonder if Joseph might have said to Jesus when he left, and to Mary, too, "Don't ever feel guilty when you can't get back. . . ?"

Father Joseph evidently let Jesus go completely, with "no strings attached"—and Mary, too, while he stayed in Nazareth "minding the store," "keeping the home fires burning"—and probably doing a bit of P. R. on behalf of Jesus and maybe even a bit of preaching and teaching as he plied his carpenter's trade—even sending whatever cash he could to Jesus and Mary, whenever he could, to help with their expenses—all that is certainly a possibility, though not recorded.

As for Jesus and Mary "keeping in touch regularly," that is not on record, either. Yet I have no doubt that Jesus fulfilled all the requirements of "Honor thy father and thy mother" that God expected, despite the fact that he probably did few of the things that people had come to expect a son to do for his parents.

"Honor thy father and thy mother" can mean many things, and not always are they the "traditional" ones that society or religious bodies lay out as the right and proper things to do. Did Jesus "honor" Joseph any less if he didn't get back to check on him, or give him a bit of help, regularly? Or did Jesus "honor" him more by assuming he could take care of himself and do it rightly and morally without Jesus there reminding him, or doing a little coaching from the sideline?

And is not the reverse true: Joseph didn't feel the need to keep checking up on Jesus, for fear that he would wander away from what was right as soon as he got out into the world and away from home and Joseph's eagle eye?

And so the "strings attached" were untied completely at both ends—in trust and love rather than in disinterest, and Joseph probably felt no more guilt because he didn't physically follow Jesus as Mary did, than Jesus and Mary felt when they didn't regularly go back to check to see if Joseph needed anything, or a helping hand, etc. Nor did Mary feel guilty because she didn't stay home and look after Joseph's needs as a wife was expected to do in those days—and is expected to do even in these days.

And so it goes—and it is well to remember this in *this* day and age when, as always, sons and daughters are expected to do what society and "religion" lay out—when mothers and fathers are expected to keep the family "together," to reel the children in with psychological "strings" if not physical—with emotional ties and bindings—like kites on a string—laying guilts on all when "traditional" expectations are deviated from.

"Untying the apron strings," the physical ones, while keeping the emotional and psychological ones tied in knots causes lots of unnecessary guilt for both parents and their adult and near-adult children, as well as an awful lot of pressure and strain and even anger for all concerned.

**EVERYBODY** wants Peace—provided, of course, it is handed to them on a silver platter, with no sweat, no strain, no pain for them.

Preachers present Peace as a gift of God only: Peace comes from God—and in a way that leads lots of people to think that God presents it on a silver platter in answer to prayer, prayer, prayer—no sweat, no strain, no pain, just prayer.

While the only thing I can find in the New Testament being presented on a silver platter is John the Baptist's severed head—with plenty of sweat and strain and pain—and a lotta blood, too, from John.

"My peace I give you—my peace I leave you" and this peace Jesus gives—leaves—caused him lottsa sweat and strain and pain—and even his life itself. And this is a part of the peace he gives—leaves—and it is passed on, not on a silver platter, but with our sweat and strain and pain—and even blood, maybe even our life itself.

Retaliation has no part in any Godly "peace plan." Jesus retaliated against none of those who did him in, or mocked him, or cried "Crucify! Crucify!" He not only forgave them from the Cross, he forgot them after Resurrection and mounted no retaliation strikes during his 40 days post-Resurrection—and left no retaliation strategy plans for his followers to carry out "in his name" after he was gone from earth.

Everybody wants to ride toward Peace in comfort—wants Peace only if it comes to them on a silver platter thanks to someone else's sweat and strain and pain—and even blood and/or death—and graciously accepts God's Peace, and Jesus' "My peace I give you

. . . leave you" as long as this is said to come to them on *Jesus'* sweat and strain and pain and blood and *not* theirs. A "cheap peace" that costs them nothing—except maybe a little prayer time, and preferably *not* on their knees.

The costs of Peace run high. Peace doesn't come cheap, nor does it come on a silver platter—nor riding on a white horse. There is no "cheap peace" any more than there is any "cheap grace" of God. The only thing that came on a silver platter in the New Testament was John's head, and that *wasn't* a "gift" of God, or Jesus, but of Herod. Jesus, nor God, present nothing "on a silver platter"—not then, nor now, nor ever.

"**CHRIST** precisely did not try to save the world by force or violence or destruction."

Copying that from where I can't remember, and I thought, God tried to save the world from sin by destroying the sinful in a flood—and it didn't work. The "righteous" he chose to carry on the human race fathered and mothered future generations as sinful, if not more so, than those God got rid of in the flood. And perhaps that is one of the reasons Jesus used no force or violence or destruction to "save" the world: because that wouldn't have worked any better for him than the flood had for God.

The flood was "force and violence and destruction" with nature as God's "sword"—and it was genocide, too. No wonder God said, "never again" and sent the rainbow. He had to watch the innocent babies and children drown right along with the sinful men and women. The flood was indiscriminate "force and violence and destruction" and God later washed his hands of that sort of thing and handed down his "Thou shalt not kill," which binds God himself to that as much as it binds Godly people—and binds, first and foremost his very own son, Jesus. Or perhaps, rather, Jesus bound himself to that of his own free will, as we who claim to be his followers must do for ourselves by renouncing any and all "force and violence and destruction!"

**Abbie Jane Wells**

**IT IS** interesting to note that Matthew gave up his tax-collecting job for Caesar in order to follow Jesus full-time; and that Zaccheus, while he didn't give up his tax-collecting job (and therefore couldn't become one of the full-time disciples), did clean up his tax-collecting act—and not in favor of himself nor Caesar, either—but in favor of the tax-payer!

And it is interesting to speculate that Zaccheus probably didn't last very long as a tax collector after that, either—about as long as it took for the news of this to reach the tax-collecting headquarters, along with the diminished tax collections that Zaccheus sent in!

"**IN MY** Father's house there are many mansions. I go to prepare a place for you."

But does he "prepare a place" for us well in advance of our natural death time, in case we get killed accidentally or from violence? And what about the megadeaths, all at one time, that would come from a nuclear holocaust? Does the influx—would the influx of millions and millions or billions in one fell swoop cause a "housing shortage" in heaven? Or are they always ready to "accommodate" as many as men and women on earth can kill, even unto the billions— modern man's military "marvels"(?) of megadeath raised to the nth degree included?

**AN IMPORTANT** thing to remember about Mary being Mother of the son of God, is that she was picked for that endeavor by God, *all by himself,* and not "hand-picked" for him by the men in charge of the religious establishment of that day! God *didn't* ask the religious establishment hierarchy: "Who do *you* think would be a woman worthy of the honor? You pick the woman *you* think should be the mother of my son—or give me a list of women *you* think are worthy for me to choose from."

No, God did his own choosing and *not* from any list presented to him by the men running the religion of that day, either! God picked a woman such as would never ever have been picked by the men running the Temple, et al, as worthy to go on *their* list of women worthy of being picked by God for anything, much less to give birth to his son. Poor, and lowly, Mary would probably have been the last Jewess the Temple crowd would have picked. She hadn't been raised in a rabbinical household and probably didn't know the ropes for measuring up to Temple and rabbinical yardsticks of what made a proper "religious" woman, according to "religious" men's rules and regulations.

Mary probably didn't measure up to the standards set by the "religious" men who were the leaders, but she measured up to the standards set by God, whatever they were, and that was good enough for God! But I doubt very much that that was ever "good" enough for the hierarchy of Mary's and Joseph's and Jesus' day. But then, neither did Joseph measure up to Temple standards for religious Jewish men. And Jesus sure never measured up to the Temple hierarchy's ideas or standards for the Messiah.

And so it went . . .

**THAT IS** *Jewish* body and blood that Jesus used bread and wine as symbols for, bread and wine left over from the Jewish Passover meal, not instead of it.

As I see it, Jesus used his hands as well as his words to point out truths; and in my mind's eye I see, as Jesus said, "As oft as you do this. . . ," his hands sweep to encompass the Passover table: "As oft as you do this Passover. . . ;" and then "do this," as he points specifically to the bread and wine, "in remembrance of me"; adding another "course" to the Passover meal, rather than a substitute for it, as a reminder: don't forget me as I am *now* in the days that are to come; don't forget *me*, the man who lived as a Jew, in the glories of the resurrected one.

*First*, he did the Passover meal in remembrance of God's Act of Deliverance, and then, with elements consecrated for the Passover meal or during the Passover meal, left-overs *from* the Passover meal, he did the bread and wine "do this in remembrance of me," an addition to the Passover meal, not a substitution or replacement for it.

Well, when I am "in charge" I may not be able to reinstate the Passover meal in the Christian calendar right away, but I *will* use matzos and kosher wine, used for the Passover meal, for the elements when I celebrate the Eucharist. I may not be able to make Easter a moveable feast, like Christmas, so that Easter always come three days after the Passover as scheduled on the Jewish calendar, as it did the *first* time around, at least not right away, but I *will* use matzos for communion wafers and kosher wine to go with that for the Eucharist as a first step and work toward Passover on The Christian church calendar on the same day it is on the Jewish calendar, with Easter three days later, with the Crucifixion properly on the day after the Passover meal.

**Abbie Jane Wells**

**PERHAPS** Jesus said ". . . I come not to bring peace . . ." because it is up to *us* to bring peace by living it. In other words, he *didn't* do it *for* us, but showed us how to do it for ourselves and for the world. Perhaps his later saying (or earlier?), "my peace I leave you," "my peace I give you" means it is there for us to "put on" by living it as he lived it—that it is an active, living role for us, not a passive "he did it for us, so we don't have to do it ourselves" thing.

Another thing: Jesus' words on the temple being destroyed in three days takes on even more meaning today, in this day of possible destruction worldwide, of churches, temples, synagogues in a nuclear holocaust. Christianity as well as Judaism—the whole list of world-wide religions and their temples, synagogues, churches, etc., will be destroyed in three days or less if push comes to shove and a nuclear holocaust is unleashed upon the earth.

And today, as religions continue to build religious structures, their members who pay the costs of this also continue to pay for, as well, the continuing building of the instruments of nuclear holocaust that will destroy the buildings they are building in the name of religion, as well as the religions themselves. And this makes absolutely no sense at all.

"I came not to bring peace but a sword"—a sword he refused to use or to allow his disciples to use even in his behalf, especially in his behalf: the first instance of "arms control" in the Christian era! As was his "one sword is enough" the first instance of "arms limitation"—a refusal to enter into any "arms race" with Caesar and his military might.

Jesus' saying, "You will hear of wars and rumors of war . . ." Could well be taken as his prophey, perhaps, of the late 20th Century communications systems, when we become almost like God and know—hear—see on TV—and read about every trouble spot and conflagration in the world—almost instantly, as it is happening.

But I cannot find where Jesus goes on to say, to instruct his followers, to *participate* in the wars and rumors they will hear of.

**Abbie Jane Wells**

**"IF JESUS** had wanted protection he could have asked God for it and let God protect him. But he does not ask God for protection. He lives and acts without protection," Dorothy Sollie writes in (*Of War and Love*, p.95).

Of course he doesn't, for he has already renounced doing that sort of thing in his response to the tempter in the desert: "If you are the Son of God, throw yourself down; for it is written:

> "He will give his angels charge over you. . . .
> 'On their hands they will bear you up, lest you
> strike your foot on a stone' . . ."

Jesus' response of ". . . shall not tempt the Lord your God" would include, I would think, when others are in the process of "throwing you down" as well as when you were tempted to do it yourself; would apply when others would "strike your whole body against a cross," rather than just when you might "strike your foot against a stone."

Besides, asking God for protection for himself, when he chose to live and act as devoid of protection as the poor people he loved did—taking a protection they sure as hell *weren't* getting from God nor anyone else, would be taking advantage of options that might well be open to him but to none else on earth.

He should ask God for a protection that God hadn't been giving to others who were in danger of being crucified or slaughtered by some other means? He should ask God for a protection he wouldn't accept from Peter? Call for legions of angels for his defense against the violence of men? For legions of angels "to bear him up," up, up and away, so that they wouldn't have to use violence to protect him from violence? Was there any way that legions of angels could protect him from the violence of men without having to use violence themselves? Without leaving his disciples and followers vulnerable to the violence he had escaped?

Calling upon God for a protection God wasn't giving to others would be setting himself apart from others—and that wasn't where it was at for Jesus—while taking what others had to take without protection from God or man was. And so Jesus ends up on a cross the same as two others did on that infamous day known as Good Friday, for Jesus had renounced calling on God for protection when the tempter tempted him to do so in the desert—and that carried through the rest of his life. He would ask from God, his father, no more than God offered to any of his children on earth—no "special dispensations," because he was his son, did Jesus ask for himself—and therein lies the reality of "he was a man for others": he chose to live like others and take what they had to take without protection from God or man. He chose to be like the poor all the way, in every way, even unto death.

**Abbie Jane Wells**

**WHILE** it may be true that Jesus, being Son of God, had some built-in protection against dental caries, and so could, all of his 33 years, say: "Look, Ma! No cavities!"; and that Mary may have gotten some kind of "special dispensation" herself because of being mother of the son of God, so that she had no dental caries: but I doubt very much that Joseph missed the dental problems that plagued the other men of his day.

It is interesting to speculate on the condition of the teeth, and other physical health, of the three members of the Holy Family, to keep it all in a down-to-earth perspective—to keep it from becoming something out-of-this-world, other worldly, unrealistic story.

I doubt very much that the Holy Family stood out in a crowd because they all had perfect teeth, undefiled by any tooth decay at all; that they never were ever ill, and that Mary and Joseph never aged at all from the moment of the conception on—though a lot of people and even artists seem to hold that view.

# The Nonviolent God

Once Jesus said, "as a good father on earth does for his children, so does God the father do, and more . . ."

And a good father on earth does not lay on his kids rules and regulations the father does not adhere to himself—a good father does not say "Do as I say, not as I do."

So when God says, "Thou shalt not kill" to his children on earth, he is as bound to obey that himself as any of his children on earth are, despite the times when humans give God credit for killing their enemies for them, or for giving them a military victory, and such things as that.

As an old tale has it: when the Israelites started to celebrate when the Red Sea closed over their Egyptians enemies, God roared: "Stop celebrating! Those are my children, too." And those who crucified the Son of God were God's children, too—and how could God save his son without killing those other children of his who were doing the violence, especially when he, too, is as bound by his "Thou shalt not kill" as was his son and everybody else?

And when Jesus didn't ask God to intervene and kill his enemies for him, to save his life, how can those who profess to follow him and who call themselves Christian, call upon God to give them a military victory when they are killing their "enemies," all of whom are also children of God as much as those who are called Christians are?

**Abbie Jane Wells**

John Donne's "Each man's death diminishes me," in its fullest sense becomes, "Each man's, woman's and child's death diminishes me." And this is as true of God and Jesus as it is for each one of us, I would think.

If man and woman were created in the "image of God"—then God's "image" is a composite of all the human beings: all men, women and children. And when humans are killed, a bit of God is destroyed, not only on earth, but in God, I would think. His image is diminished, a la John Donne's "Each . . . death diminishes me."

**RATHER** than a doctrine of "Original Sin," it well could be that it is "Original Stupidity" that the human race is afflicted with, infected with! The refusal of many to take new looks at old man-made precepts, premises, theories, doctrines, etc., is plain stupid. A lot of usable knowledge is available now that wasn't around when old, traditional, and orthodox ideas were formed; and so no man-formulated or woman-formulated ideas remain true forever. Each generation has to think anew for itself, and that includes re-thinking what has come from others now, or in other times.

Jesus' "Who do they say I am?" to Peter was followed by, after Peter told him who "they" said he was, Jesus', "But who do *you* say I am?" or, in other words, "Think for yourself, Peter, don't just take what others say and let it go at that." And that's a good rule-of-thumb for all of us to follow.

"Read, mark, and inwardly digest, and see what the Scriptures say to *you*," and heavy on the YOU.

There is more than meets the eye in all of the Scriptures. Like the passage about Jesus at the Temple when he was age 13. When he stayed there with the teachers, and Mary and Joseph looked everywhere for him and finally found him in the Temple. "And Mary pondered these things in her heart," and I'll bet she pondered a lot more than just this and Jesus' "Did you not know that I must be about my Father's business?"

I think Mary, and Joseph, too, and no doubt Jesus, too, pondered a lot about the: "Sitting among the teachers, listening to them and asking them questions; and all who heard him were amazed at his understanding and his answers." The Temple teachers were "amazed at his understanding and answers," and you would think, wouldn't you, that they would have wanted him to stay at the Temple as a student? What a student to have! A student who "amazed" you with his (or her) understanding and answers is every teacher's dream of a student, isn't it? Yet the Temple teachers didn't seem to want Jesus as their student, certainly offered no entreaties or incentives. Their willingness to let him leave and go back to Nazareth with Mary and Joseph is much like unto being rejected by rabbinical school, or seminary, *after* "taking entrance exams" and making all A + s, isn't it?

I think this is one of the things Mary "pondered in her heart," along with what Jesus did, and said to her. She must have pondered as well what the Temple teachers said and did—or didn't do. "Actions speak louder than words," and the "amazed" Temple teachers didn't follow through on their "amazement" with his understanding and answers—no "scholarship" did they offer so that Jesus could stay at the Temple *with them*. Instead they let him leave with Mary and Joseph, literally sending him to a "trade school" to learn carpentering with Joseph, rather than keeping him at their "professional school" to study with them.

Well, if you *don't* think Mary, and Joseph, too, pondered *that* in their hearts, then you don't know much about poor parents of an amazing child—*any* amazing "in understanding and answers" child who is rejected by the very teachers who find him (her) amazing, and consigned to a less than full use of his/her capabilities. There is a lot for all of us to ponder in this—and here, too, Jesus' "As you have done it to the least of these, you have done it unto me" applies, as schools and our society often offer few if any opportunities to the children of poor parents, despite their "amazing" capabilities.

**I WONDER** how long Mary had to wear the clothes she traveled to Bethlehem in—took with her to Bethlehem? I wonder how long Joseph had to make do with the clothes he had on, or had with him for the trip to Bethlehem?

"Rise, take the child and his mother and flee to Egypt. . . ," and with only what they had brought with them from Nazareth! Plus, of course, the gifts the wise men brought. I wonder if they were as sparsely clad, as devoid of extras, as the disciples Jesus would send out later with "no bag for your journey, nor two tunics or sandals, nor a staff. . . ?" Could it be that Jesus thought then: "If I can do it—if father Joe and mom could do it when they hurried to Egypt, then these should be able to do it" when he sent the 12 out with only the clothes on their backs and the sandals on their feet.

Of course, Mary and Joseph *did* have the wise men's gifts with them; that is, they did unless they left them in the stable in their haste to get out of Bethlehem as fast as they could! And that would be understandable, for they sure weren't used to having gold and frankinsense and myrrh around to look after—and they may have remembered the Christmas gifts the Babe got *after* they were too far away to go back for them. Packing up to leave under the threat of a fast-coming violence must be a lot like leaving a burning house in a hurry, with only what you are wearing and what you can grab on the way out—and the kid or kids—giving little thought to saving the family heirlooms or valuables—remembering them when it is too dangerous to go back for them. And going back for anything the Holy Family had left behind in Bethlehem, even the wise men's valuable gifts, had they been left behind, would have been foolish and dangerous.

And, "Rise, take the Child and his Mother and flee . . ." Well, you don't think real clearly at a time like that, any more than you do if you wake up from a sound sleep to find the house is on fire, that's for sure—and Mary and Joseph and the Babe could well have fled with only what they had been sleeping in, with no thought of taking anything more than what they could grab in a hurry as they left the stable.

So they, too, may have set out on their journey to Egypt with "no gold or silver or copper in their belts," just like the disciples Jesus sent out later, and without the rich gifts of the wise men, either!

However it really happened, it was a setting forth on a journey they had not prepared themselves for when they were getting ready to leave Nazareth for their comparatively short trip to Bethlehem. All the way to Egypt with only what they had with them in Bethlehem—a really "down-to-bare-bones" trip, if ever there was one! And only shortly after Mary had given birth, too—Mary still wearing the maternity clothes she had traveled to Bethlehem in, though now carrying the Babe in her arms rather than in her womb. Refugees now; political refugees with a price on the head of the Babe—a price the innocent boy babes in Bethlehem would have to pay instead.

The days after Christmas for Mary and Joseph were fearful and harrowing days, for this was no planned in advance vacation trip South for rest and recreation, and that's for damn sure!

I wonder how long it was before Mary could get out of those maternity clothes and Joseph could get out of his traveling clothes—which must have been almost in shreds by the time they reached Egypt—to say nothing of what the Babe's swaddling clothes must have been like by then.

This is but another instance of being sent out from the familiar through the desert to seek a new place, this time only a temporary place, not for forever like Sarah and Abraham—and then Hagar and Ishmael—and much later the Israelites. Away from the familiar and into the unknown and the new, occurs time after time to different persons and peoples throughout biblical history, and even unto today, and into the unknown future times.

**I HAVE** been picking around at the wise men—picking them to pieces mentally and on paper. Something about them bothered me: I didn't think it an exemplary thing that they went back on their word to Herod. I didn't think that their dream to return to their home by another way was a dream sent by God. (Psalm 15's "Lord who shall dwell in thy tabernacle? . . . He that sweareth unto his neighbor, and disappointeth him not, though it were to his own hindrance. . . ." kept getting in the way of that.)

And I kept thinking that their running out on Herod might have caused a good bit of Herod's anger—as Matthew 2:16 puts it: "Then Herod, when he saw that he had been tricked by the wise men, was in a furious rage, and he sent and killed all the male children in Bethlehem who were two years and under. . . ."—and so contributed to the slaughter of the innocents.

Well, I've sort of been barking up the wrong tree all these years—or up *one* tree, as if it were the only tree to bark up! Picking at what the wise men did *after* they had seen the Christ Child, without giving a thought to what they did *before* they saw the Christ Child.

Then—reading John Fry's essay in October, 1983 *Frying Pan*, where he writes about Jesus telling his disciples to "shut up about this Jesus thing," telling those he healed to tell no one. "He told his disciples and the people he healed to keep their traps shut," writes Fry.

And then he drops the blockbuster, for me at least, with his:

> "And remember if the Magi hadn't blabbered all they knew the massacre of the innocents never would have taken place."

I'll buy that! But since the wise men *did* blabber all they knew to Herod, I won't toss out all my meanderings of mind about the wise men chickening out on returning to Herod as they promised as also a contributing cause for the slaughter of the Bethlehem Babes.

"Loose lips" not only sink ships, they can, and often do, cause the death of the innocent; Fry's "... if the Magi hadn't blabbered all they knew the massacre of the innocents never would have taken place," being a case in point—and I am forever grateful to John Fry for bringing this to my attention, and I gladly pass it on!

**THE CHURCH** celebrates, with no holds barred, the Christmas Birth—and Easter's Resurrection—but there is no like festive occasion for the *first* act of God upon which they both depend: the Conception. The Church tends to downplay the fact that without the first act of God in the Conception, there would be no Christmas and no Easter—for what has not been conceived cannot be born or resurrected—or crucified either.

Yet the first Act of God on which the birth, the life, the death, the resurrection of Jesus depend isn't given any billing at all by way of a celebration comparable to Christmas and Easter.

The "Christmas era" started nine months before the Christmas Birth, with the Conception. Jesus was son of God in utero as well as after death and more impressively so (at least for some) after Resurrection. It may have taken the Resurrection to show the world—and the doubters—that Jesus was the son of God—but it only took the Conception for Mary and Joseph, and Elizabeth, too, to know this—and later, 30 or more years later, for the disciples and other followers to become aware of this.

This is no "which came first, the chicken or the egg?" sort of thing. The act of God in the Conception came first, and without it there would have been no second act of God in the Resurrection, re: Jesus—no Easter—and no Christmas either, or Good Friday.

And if the Conception were given the proper billing—with the Church year starting with *this* event—with celebration to at least match those of Christmas

**Abbie Jane Wells**

and Easter, it would not be possible, or so I think, for
anyone to wonder if "we too often have all but forgotten the real father," for he would be right there,
front and center, along with Mary, from the first
crack out of the box: rather than off hidden in the
wings somewhere waiting for people to "stop and
think about it, and then like a dawning light . . .
realize 'of course! That's where it all begins . . .'"

# A bunch of tid-bits to chew on:

Jesus created a "lowerarchy"—sure as hell *didn't* create any "hierarchy" with his "and the first shall be last and the last shall be first"; and "as you have done it to the *least* of these, you have done it unto me"; and "take the lowest seat at the table rather than the highest . . ."

\*  \*  \*

Paul's "thorns of the flesh" could well have been plantars warts! They are sure "thorns of the flesh"—especially if you have 'em in the balls of the feet and have to do as much walking as Paul had to do! And in an age where there were no podiatrists handy, even if you could afford one!!

\*  \*  \*

Jesus said: "In heaven they neither marry nor are given in marriage"—and some assume that means that everyone in heaven will be sexless, and some have assumed that all in heaven will be transformed into one sex: male. But Jesus *didn't* go on to say, "Therefore there will be no sex." He only said there is no marriage—so who is to say that heaven isn't a place of "Swinging Singles" ("swinging" responsibly, of course). Who knows? Could be!

**Abbie Jane Wells**

**JESUS'** refusal to condemn the woman caught in the very act of adultery is usually seen as Jesus' love for her and for all weak and sinful human beings. Completely overlooked most of the time is the justice contained in his refusal to condemn the woman, and that this would be justice, pure and simple, even if there had been no love attached.

For that woman caught in the very act of adultery wasn't the only one caught in the act; she was just the only one the men brought before Jesus for judgment: they had let her partner get away! Get off the hook! For one is never caught in the act of adultery alone.

The men evidently "forgave" the man his part in the act—they sure as hell didn't bring *him* before Jesus for judgment—and how could a just Jesus condemn the woman *and not her partner,* as those men expected him to? As the men themselves had done?

So we have *these people* caught in the act of adultery—the man who got away as well as the woman the men "caught," for, believe you me, that woman *didn't* do it all alone by herself!

It is easy to understand that if Jesus did happen to say to the men who brought the woman before him, "And where is her partner?", or "and which one of you was her partner?" that *those* words might get lost in the recording of the event by men with a First Century mind-set. It was the *woman* the men thought deserving of stoning, not her male partner, as it has been the woman who down through history who has been marked with the Scarlet Letter, not her male partner; and as it is the prostitute who serves the jail sentence, not her male customer.

139

Jesus cut through this double standard of "justice"(?) when he refused to condemn the woman for her part in an act of adultery—knowing full well, I am sure, for he sure wasn't blind or stupid and oblivious to the facts of life, that: "There were two at that party!" though only one of them was brought to be judged.

Reading between the lines of Scripture brings out lottsa interesting details that got left out of the written record, whether accidentally or on purpose there is no way to know—but the Scriptures are all written by men and sometimes they don't see the details, or don't want to see the details, that women, or some women, are more prone to notice.

And so it goes, even today.

"To the Galatians Paul wrote 'When the time had fully come God sent forth His son' (Gal. 4:40). God times his movements so that his purpose can be accomplished through human efforts." [said Clinton Marsh] Had Jesus come to a different people in a different place at a different time could as much have been accomplished?"

From "To Study War No More"
—Linda Miller

**PAUL** as well as Clinton Marsh and just about everybody else tends to forget that it took a "yes" from Mary *before* God could "sent forth his Son"—and if there is any truth to that "when the time had fully come," it is that *Mary's* time had come when she went into labor at the end of her pregnancy: *that's* when the time had fully come—*that* is when Jesus's time to be born had fully come!

As for "Had Jesus come to a different people in a different place at a different time. . . ," I don't think you can juggle his place in history—or Mary's—that way; and since Jesus *was* born of Mary, you'd have to get her as well as Jesus into "a different people in a different place at a different time—which isn't humanly, or Godly, possible.

Of course, it *is* possible for God to have a Son of a woman "in a different people in a different place at a different time"—but *that* son wouldn't be Jesus, for Jesus was Mary's son as well as God's—which lottsa people tend to forget at times.

For all I know—for all anybody knows—God may

have "proposed" (or propositioned?) to many women he thought likely mothers for his son down through the ages but, *as far as we know,* Mary was the first one to say an unqualified "yes" and the only one to say "yes."

"When the time had fully come, God sent forth his son"—and the "Time had fully come" only because the woman Mary said "yes." "God times his movements. . . ?" He "times" them according to the responses he gets from humans, if the "yes" from Mary is an example, and I would say that it is one of the prime examples. "God waited patiently" (and maybe from creation itself?) for a woman to say "yes" so that he could have a son he could send forth—as patiently as he "waited for people to bring forth women's suffrage, child labor laws and the abolition of slavery . . ." and as patiently as he is "waiting for someone"—for lottsa someones—"to move to study war no more."

In fact—Jesus' "time had come" is even more specific than just when Mary said "yes"—it was the specific time Mary said "yes"—a month earlier or a month later and God's son—though son of Mary— would not have been Jesus—for Jesus, like all of us, was the product of one particular ovum, at that short moment in time when ripe for conception. We each have our "moment in time," and one moment only, and so it was for Jesus. And if that ovum is not fertilized, our moment would have been gone forever—though other children are possibilities with each and every fertile time of the mother.